KEN GRIFFEY, JR.:
SUPERSTAR CENTERFIELDER

John Rolfe
Scott Gramling
Jon Kramer

Sports Illustrated
FOR
KiDS
BOOKS

This Library Edition First Published and Exclusively Distributed by
The Rosen Publishing Group, Inc.
New York

This book is about a son and his father, but I am dedicating it to three wonderful mothers: My wife, Victoria Anne, the mother of four great kids: Sean, Colin, Amber, and Jesse; my mother, Jeanette Rolfe, without whom I wouldn't have been possible (Thanks, Muzz!); my late mother-in-law, Winifred Mary Wragge, who welcomed me into her family with open arms. – John Rolfe

To my beautiful wife, Lisa, whose love and support provide me with the strength and confidence to accomplish the things I do. – Scott Gramling

This library edition first published in 2003 and exclusively distributed by The Rosen Publishing Group, Inc., New York

Book Design: Michelle Innes
Additional editorial material: Nel Yomtov

Photo Credits: Cover, p. 1 © John Cordes/Icon SMI; pp 5, 35, 57 © ALLSPORT; pp. 13, 25, 73, 79, 87, 107, 131 © VJ Lovero/Icon SMI; p. 63 © Reuters NewMedia Inc./CORBIS; p. 95 © AFP/CORBIS; p. 119 © Bettmann/CORBIS

First edition

Library of Congress Cataloging-in-Publication Data

Rolfe, John.
  Ken Griffey, Jr. : superstar centerfielder / John Rolfe, Scott Gramling, and Jon Kramer.– 1st ed.
      p. cm.
Summary: Details the life and career of Ken Griffey, Jr., highlighting his relationship with his baseball player father and also his experiences with the Seattle Mariners.
Includes bibliographical references and index.
  ISBN 0-8239-3687-2 (lib. bdg.)
  1. Griffey, Ken, Jr.–Juvenile literature. 2. Baseball players–United States–Biography–Juvenile literature. [1. Griffey, Ken, Jr. 2. Baseball players. 3. African Americans–Biography.] I. Gramling, Scott. II. Kramer, Jon. III. Title.
  GV865.G69 R66 2003
  796.357'092–dc21
                                        2001008717

CONTENTS

>> MASTER BLASTER

Ken Griffey, Jr. walked to the plate at Coors Field, in Denver, Colorado. It was the fourth inning of a game between Junior's Cincinnati Reds and the Colorado Rockies. The date was April 10, 2000.

That was a special day for Junior and his family. Junior's dad — Ken Griffey, Sr. — was celebrating his 50th birthday. Junior was playing in only his seventh game as a Red, and he was just one home run away from hitting the 400th homer of his career. Only 26 players in major league history had ever hit 400 homers.

As Junior settled in at home plate that afternoon, his dad watched from the dugout. Ken, Sr. had played 12 seasons with the Reds. Now he was their bench coach.

Colorado pitcher Rolando Arrojo threw two balls. Junior dug in. He expected Rolando to throw a strike after missing with his first two pitches. Sure enough, the pitch was over the plate. Junior blasted the ball into the leftfield stands, 378 feet away.

Junior was 30 years 141 days old. That made him the youngest player to reach 400 career home runs. He broke the record set by Hall of Fame slugger Jimmie Foxx. Jimmie was 30 years 248 days when he hit his 400th for the Boston Red Sox, in 1938. Hank Aaron, baseball's all-time homer king with 755 career dingers, didn't reach 400 until he was 32 years 74 days old.

A PAIR OF GRIFFEYS

Junior was thrilled that he had delivered his big blow on his dad's birthday. "It's a cheap way of not buying him a gift," he joked to reporters after the game. But Junior must be on to something. It was the *fourth* time that he had homered on his dad's birthday. He also did it in 1994, 1992, and 1989.

Hitting number 400 as a Reds player made the event especially meaningful for Junior. He grew up in Cincinnati, Ohio. His dad was a speedy rightfielder who helped the Reds win the World Series in 1975 and 1976. Ken, Sr. played 19 seasons (from 1973 through 1991) in the big leagues for the Reds, New York Yankees, Atlanta Braves, and Seattle Mariners. He was a three-time All-Star and the MVP of the 1980 All-Star Game.

Junior and his dad made history in 1989 when they became the first father and son to play in the major leagues at the same time. Junior was with the Seattle Mariners and his dad played for the Braves. The next year, Ken, Sr. joined the Mariners, and the Griffeys got to play on the same major league team.

They enjoyed two seasons as teammates before Ken, Sr. retired as a player, after the 1991 season. He became a coach with the Mariners and moved on to the Reds in November 1996.

Junior, meanwhile, became the best player in major league baseball. He spent 11 seasons with the Mariners and whacked 40 or more homers six times, topping 50 in a season twice (1997 and 1998). He also won 10 American League Gold Glove awards. (A Gold Glove is awarded to the best defensive player at each position.)

But Junior always hoped to join his dad again someday. After the 1999 season, he finally did. He asked the Mariners to trade him. He was overjoyed when they sent him to the Reds, on February 10, 2000. He signed a nine-year, $116.5 million contract, and the team flew their new star to Cincinnati for a news conference.

Cincinnati embraced its hometown hero. Some 2,000 fans greeted Junior at the airport. When he appeared at Cinergy Field for the news conference, his dad stood next to him with an ear-to-ear grin.

"I'm finally home," Junior said. "I'm happy to be here. This is something you dream about as a little kid, and I finally did it."

If Junior was excited, how do you think the people of Cincinnati felt? Thousands of them called the Reds office to buy tickets to home games. There were so many calls that the team had to put in more phone lines! Fans wanted anything that had the name GRIFFEY on it. They eagerly snapped up T–shirts, uniform jerseys, baseballs, caps, and whatever else was available.

The Reds opened the 2000 season at home on April 3 against the Milwaukee Brewers. It was a damp day, but that didn't matter. The 55,596 fans in the stands at Cinergy Field gave Junior a loud standing ovation when he was introduced during pre–game ceremonies. He popped up in the first inning and grounded out two innings later. The game was called because of rain in the top of the sixth inning with the score tied at 3–3.

Junior struggled in the next five games. Perhaps he was trying too hard to get off to a hot start and prove himself in the glare of all the attention. Or maybe he just needed time to get used to National League pitching. Whatever the reason, Junior had only three hits — and just one homer — in 26 at–bats when he arrived at Coors Field on April 10. But with one swing of his bat that day, he took another step toward the Hall of Fame.

THE BEST IN THE GAME?

Many fans think that Junior is the best all–around player in baseball. Many players and managers agree. Junior's peers chose him as the Player of the Decade for the 1990s.

"All around, I would say he's the best, and his defense is incredible," says All–Star slugger Frank Thomas of the Chicago White Sox.

"When you look at what Junior has done and the skills he possesses, you have to say that in this era he is as good as anyone who has played," says Lou Piniella, who started managing the Mariners in 1992. "I can't think of any player in the past thirty years to compare with Junior." Before he was a manager, Lou played in the majors for more than 17 years.

You could say that Junior's awesome baseball talent "runs in the family." Junior's dad, of course, is quite impressed with Junior, too. "Like everyone else, I am amazed," he says. "I'm in awe of him. He's doing things I could never do."

Junior is often compared to such Hall of Fame players as Willie Mays, Joe DiMaggio, and Ted Williams. Willie was a speedy, slugging centerfielder who was nicknamed "The Say Hey Kid." Joe was called "The Yankee Clipper" because of his fielding grace with the New York Yankees. Ted Williams batted .406 in 1941 and is the last player to bat .400 or higher in a season.

Junior makes everything he does look easy. Most players spend about five years in the minor leagues before they reach the majors. Junior spent only two before he made the Mariners' roster in spring training before the 1989 season.

Junior thinks people make baseball too complicated. "You hit the ball, you run, you go after it, and you catch it," he says. "You might not be able to figure out what pitch the

WHAT'S IN A NUMBER?

Junior wore jersey number 24 with the Mariners but had to switch when he was traded to the Reds in February 2000. Number 24 had belonged to Cincinnati first baseman Tony Perez for 16 seasons. Tony was elected to the Hall of Fame in 1999, and the Reds had decided to honor him by retiring his number. So Junior decided to wear number 30, his dad's number. Ken, Sr. happily switched to number 33.

guy's going to throw you, but eventually, he has to throw something across the plate that I can hit. It's a simple game, really. I was born with this talent. I can't help it if I make things look easy that some people think are difficult."

Former Baltimore Oriole third baseman Cal Ripken, Jr. is a future Hall of Famer. Still, he marvels at Junior: "All of us would like to be able to keep the game that simple, but only players with unbelievable natural talent can just go out and do the things Junior does."

SUPER-POPULAR

Fans love to watch all that natural talent at work. Junior is one of those rare athletes — like Michael Jordan — that fans in *every* city will root for.

In 1990, Junior became the first Mariner in history to be chosen by fans to start in the All-Star Game. In 1994, he received more All-Star votes (6,079,688) from fans than any player ever.

A big reason fans love Junior so much is that he always looks as if he's having fun. He wears his cap backward during warm-ups. His face is often lit up by a beaming smile. He loves clowning around, listening to rap music, and playing video games.

Junior's talent and personality have made him well-known outside of baseball. In 1994, he appeared in the movie *Little Big League.* He makes commercials and endorses products for Upper Deck sports cards, Nintendo video games, and Nike athletic equipment. His picture graced a box of Wheaties cereal in 2000.

Like many super-popular athletes, Junior has learned that being famous isn't easy. He is constantly mobbed by fans and asked for interviews by reporters. In 1993, he had to move to a new house because fans found out where he lived and were knocking on his door all the time. More than anything, Junior wants a peaceful life for his wife, Melissa, their son, Trey, and their daughter, Taryn. He can be quiet around reporters and fans, but he treats people with courtesy and respect as long as they treat him the same way.

Respect comes to those who hit 400 home runs. Junior joined some of the all-time greats when he belted the ball out of Coors Field on that April day in Denver, Colorado. What better present could a kid give his father?

>> THE KID

George Kenneth Griffey, Jr. was born on November 21, 1969, in Donora, Pennsylvania. He was the first of Ken and Alberta Griffey's three children. A younger brother, Craig, was born a year and a half later and a younger sister, Lathesia, came along two years after Craig.

Donora is a town of about 7,500 people located near the city of Pittsburgh, in southwestern Pennsylvania. It is famous for being the birthplace of Baseball Hall of Fame outfielder Stan Musial. Stan the Man, as he is called, played for the St. Louis Cardinals from 1941 to 1963. Ken Griffey, Sr. was also born in Donora. *His* dad, Buddy, played baseball with Stan the Man in high school. In Donora, Ken, Sr. also met his future wife, Alberta, who is known as "Birdie."

When Junior was born, Ken, Sr. was just beginning his first season of professional baseball, with a Cincinnati Reds minor league team. His salary was only $500 per month, so he had to do odd jobs during the off-season

to make ends meet. When no work was available, the Griffeys received money from the government in the form of welfare payments.

Ken, Sr. tried hard to be a good father. His own dad had left home when Ken, Sr. was only two years old. Growing up without his dad made Ken, Sr. want to be the father to his kids that he never had.

"Hopefully, I did a good enough job that they know right from wrong," he says.

AN EARLY ACHIEVER

Junior showed signs of physical talent at a very early age. He started walking when he was only seven months old. Most babies don't start to walk until they are about 12 months old.

Junior's dream of being a major leaguer like his dad began as soon as he learned how to play baseball, at age four or five. But Ken, Sr. never forced his children to play sports.

"I don't believe in pressuring kids," Ken, Sr. says. "I told the boys, 'If you want to play, if you need some help, let me know.' With Junior, you could see it was what he wanted and how much fun he was having playing it. Craig didn't like the game. There was no reason to force it on him."

Junior also played football, basketball, and soccer with Craig when they got older. Football was Craig's favorite sport. He later went on to play defensive back at Ohio State University. After college, he switched to baseball and was an outfielder in the Mariners' minor league system from 1991 to 1997. Then he signed a minor league contract with the Cincinnati Reds.

BIG-LEAGUE DAD

Ken, Sr. made the Cincinnati Reds major league team in 1973 and started to make a lot more money. He moved the family to Cincinnati, where they lived in a nice house in the suburb of Mount Airy. The house had a big family room with a spot for Ken, Sr. to display his trophies. The basement had an exercise room with weight machines.

Ken, Sr. quickly became an important player for the famous Reds teams of the 1970s. These teams were known as "The Big Red Machine" because of their powerful hitters. During the 1970s, the Reds won six National League West division titles. They won the World Series in 1975 and 1976.

Ken, Sr. batted over .300 in both of those World Series championship years, and he made more money than ever before. He bought a Rolls Royce. Junior sometimes showed up for his Little League games in the Rolls, driven by his mom! When Junior turned 16, in 1988, his dad bought him an expensive BMW car. "My dad would give you the shirt off his back," Junior says. "I was spoiled."

Ken, Sr. agrees. "Junior was spoiled," he says. "But I didn't mind spoiling him. A lot of things he did, I didn't get a chance to do when I was that age."

Having a dad who was a big-league ballplayer gave Junior the chance to do many things most kids never get to do. He hung out at the ballpark with his dad, met famous players, and played on the field with their sons. He went to the World Series in 1975, when he was five.

Junior says he was never awed by the players many people worshipped as heroes. "They were just people my dad worked with," Junior says. "I didn't walk around thinking, 'Wow, these are the Cincinnati Reds.' My dad told me, 'Don't copy them. Just be yourself.'"

Junior says he never thought of his dad as a major league star. If you talk to his mom, though, she'll tell you Junior was impressed by his dad all the time. She says he knew what his dad's batting average was on any given day and that Junior got upset whenever the Reds lost.

When Junior and his dad played catch in the backyard, sometimes mom joined in the fun. Birdie was a good athlete. She had played basketball and volleyball when she was in high school and later won a home-run-hitting contest against the wives of other players.

"She used to play catch with me, but one day I threw hard and smoked her hand," Junior says. "She threw down the glove, and that was the last time she caught for me!"

Junior had a lot of natural talent for baseball. He also benefited by being able to watch his dad play. "I watched my dad play for years," he says. "I talked to him every day about the game. There isn't one thing I've seen so far that he hasn't told me about before."

Junior started playing Little League baseball when he was eight. He and Craig were teammates that year on the Mount Airy team in the Knothole League. Craig played centerfield and back-up catcher. Junior pitched and often threw so hard that kids went to bat in tears because they were so afraid of being hit by a pitch.

Once Junior got started in Little League, Ken, Sr. did not interfere with his son's coaches. He let them decide what to teach Junior. Ken, Sr.'s biggest efforts were at instilling confidence in Junior.

"I always talked to Kenny about his mental outlook," Ken, Sr. says. "Questions like, 'How positive are you about yourself?' 'How much confidence do you have in yourself and what you want to do?' I always told him that no one was ever going to hit, run, and throw for him. You have to have confidence in those things."

Most of all, Ken, Sr. made sure that his son did not take baseball too seriously. "[Dad] always used to tell me to go out and have fun, no matter what," Junior says.

Junior became so good by the time he was 11 that his dad could not strike him out. Junior got so used to success that failure took him by complete surprise.

In one Little League game, he hit a hard shot, but the ball was caught by the first baseman. "I cried so hard they had to take me out of the game," Junior says.

▶ TIME CAPSULE 1979

IN 1979, THE YEAR JUNIOR TURNED 10 YEARS OLD:

▶ The Pittsburgh Pirates defeated the Baltimore Orioles in the World Series, four games to three.

▶ Israel and Egypt signed the Camp David peace treaty.

▶ Iranian militants took over the U.S. Embassy in Teheran and held 53 Americans hostage for 444 days.

▶ Baggy pants and roller skating were hot fads.

▶ The first Sony Walkman tape player was introduced.

▶ Disco music was popular.

Birdie rushed over and tried to comfort her son, "Look, your father makes plenty of outs," she said. "One out is not going to make any difference."

Junior looked at his mom and cried, "But that's him — that's not me!"

LIFE IN THE BIG APPLE

The Griffeys' lives changed in 1981. Less than three weeks before Junior's twelfth birthday, the Reds traded Ken, Sr. to the New York Yankees. The Griffey family stayed in Cincinnati, so Junior didn't get to see his dad very much during the baseball season.

While his dad was away, Junior kept in touch by talking with him on the phone. It became a habit, one that Junior became known for after he began his own pro career.

During the season, Junior and his family occasionally visited Dad in New York City. Junior made some friends on the Yankees. One of them was outfielder Rickey Henderson. Rickey became Junior's favorite player, and they even played one-on-one basketball together.

"Rickey gave me my first talk about baseball other than my father," Junior says. "He told me, 'You're going to be here in the majors someday. Stay away from the wrong crowd. If somebody does drugs, his name may not be mentioned, but yours will.'"

During those visits to Yankee Stadium, Junior and his dad went to the ballpark to work out in the outfield and take batting practice, just as they had done in Cincinnati. Junior made an impression on his father's Yankee teammates. They could tell he was going to be special.

"As a fifteen-year-old, Junior walked around with that little bit of a swagger," says Scott Bradley, who played for the Yankees in 1985 and later became Junior's teammate on the Mariners. "He knew how good he was."

By age 16, Junior was good enough to compete against 18-year-olds in Connie Mack League baseball. (Connie Mack is a league for kids ages 18 and under.) In the 1986 Connie Mack World Series, Junior hit three homers in one game: one to leftfield, one to center, and one to right.

Birdie kept telling Ken, Sr. how good Junior was, but he had a hard time believing it because he was able to go to only a few of Junior's games between 1981 and 1988.

As a teenager, Ken, Jr. had a complete case of sports on the brain. Unfortunately, he didn't pay much attention to his schoolwork. Junior's grades were so bad that when he entered Archbishop Moeller High School, he had to sit out his freshman year of baseball. Then he missed his sophomore season because he decided to go to spring training in Florida with his dad.

HIGH SCHOOL STANDOUT

It wasn't until his junior season that Ken, Jr. finally began to play high school baseball. That is very late for anyone who hopes to make it to the majors, but Junior made up for lost time during his first year of high school sports. He batted .478 with 11 homers. He grew six inches to 6 feet 3 inches, and gained 40 pounds. His new size also helped make him a star wide receiver on the school football team.

OH! IT'S OHIO!

Ohio, the state where Junior grew up, is the birthplace of professional baseball. The 1869 Cincinnati Red Stockings was the first team to pay its players. The state gets its name from an Iroquois Indian word that means "something great." Ohio became America's seventeenth state in 1803. Ohio is called "the Mother of Presidents." Seven U.S. Presidents were born there: Ulysses S. Grant, Rutherford B. Hayes, James Garfield, Benjamin Harrison, William McKinley, William Howard Taft, and Warren G. Harding.

Junior's dislike of being tackled made him decide to quit football his senior year, even though the team had won the Ohio State championship the year before. It also made more sense for him to concentrate on baseball because he had so much talent.

Mike Cameron, Junior's high school baseball coach, says Junior was the best player he ever coached during his 20 years at Moeller High. That's a big compliment. Several major league stars, such as Reds shortstop Barry Larkin, have played at Moeller.

Junior belted three home runs in one game and set a school record with 20 career homers during his two seasons at Moeller. He was also a dazzling fielder who could catch long fly balls while running full speed with his back to home plate. Major league scouts were wild about Junior, but the attention he received from them did not faze him at all. But, that is *not* to say he was never fazed.

"Only when his father was there would Kenny pressure himself," Coach Cameron says. "A hundred scouts could be in the stands and it wouldn't make a difference. But not his father."

Junior could not seem to get a hit when his dad was watching. "When he was there, it was the only time I thought I had to impress somebody," Junior says.

In his senior year, Junior set a school record by batting .478, and had seven homers and 28 RBIs in 24 games. He also stole 13 bases without being thrown out. Mariner scouts graded Junior's talent and gave him scores between 63 and 73. In their grading system, a score between 50 and 59 meant a player had the potential to be an All–Star.

On June 2, 1987, when he was 17, the Mariners made Junior the first player chosen in the major league draft of amateur players. He was the first son of a major league player to be chosen first. Junior had also received a scholarship offer from Florida State University, but he wasn't about to turn down pro ball — not after the Mariners chose him first!

With his dad acting as his agent, Junior agreed to a minor league contract that paid him a bonus of $160,000 just to sign the paper! Mariner officials then told Junior, "We want you in the majors in three years."

Making the majors that quickly is tough, but as it turned out, the Mariners didn't have to wait too long.

>> NEW KID ON THE BLOCK

The beginning of Junior's pro career planted the seed of a dream in his father's mind. Would it be possible that one day they might be able to play in the major leagues together?

It wasn't likely to happen. At the time, Ken, Sr. was 37 years old. He had been traded to the Atlanta Braves in 1986 and the end of his career was in sight. Few players are still physically able to play in the majors after 35. Even so, Ken, Sr. told his son, "You hurry up and I'll try to hang on. Maybe we can play together."

Ken, Sr. knew that life in the minor leagues would be a big adjustment for Junior, who had never lived away from home before. Ken, Sr. told reporters, "If he has any problems, he can give me a call. I'll call him every day, too, to make sure he's all right."

The Mariners sent Junior to their Rookie League team, in Bellingham, Washington. (Rookie League is the lowest level of minor league baseball.) Bellingham is about 90 miles north of Seattle. His first hit was a home run.

Junior's team often took long bus rides (some up to 10 hours) to play in the neighboring states of Oregon and Idaho. The team bus was almost 30 years old. It had no bathroom and was very uncomfortable. On Junior's first long trip, he coped with the boredom and discomfort by climbing into the overhead luggage rack and going to sleep.

There were all kinds of surprises and trouble waiting for Junior that season. He had run-ins with the teenage sons of the team's bus driver. Junior told reporters that one of them called him "nigger" and another went looking for him with a gun. He was finding his new life in the minors to be pretty miserable.

"To be honest with you, it was a whole lot worse than I ever imagined," Junior says. "I didn't know what to do. All I knew is I wanted to go home."

Junior turned to his family for support. He started calling home so much his phone bill was $600 a month. His unhappiness affected his performance on the field. He fell into a slump and when his batting average dropped to .230, his mom flew to Bellingham.

Birdie was unhappy to learn that Junior had been benched for breaking a team rule against staying out too late at night and that he was thinking about quitting.

"I knew he needed some sympathy, but I got mad and told him to concentrate on his career," Birdie says. She gave him a piece of her mind. "The night before I left, I gave it to him up one side and down the other. He didn't call me for four days."

Rick Sweet, the team's manager, said Junior needed to grow up and keep his mind on the game. Junior often failed to hustle or lazily caught fly balls with one hand.

Junior agreed. "I have to mature," he said "That's why I'm here."

And mature he did: He finished the season as the team's leader in batting average (.313), homers (14), and RBIs (43). *Baseball America* magazine rated him as the number–one prospect in the minor leagues.

Junior's first season of pro ball ended better than it had begun, but the rocky times continued. When he returned home, he began having arguments with his dad. Now that Junior was a professional, Ken, Sr. expected his son to act more grown up and be responsible.

"Dad wanted me to pay rent or get my own place," Junior later told reporter Bob Finnigan of the *Seattle Times* newspaper in 1992. "I was confused. I was hurting and I wanted to cause some hurt for others."

Junior told the reporter that in January 1988, he tried to kill himself by swallowing 277 aspirin tablets. Junior's girlfriend and her brother tried to stop him from taking the pills, but were unsuccessful. Junior then got into his car, but threw up before he could drive away. His girlfriend's mother drove him to the hospital.

Afterward, Junior and his dad worked out their differences by having long heart–to–heart talks. Junior later decided to talk to a reporter about the incident because he hoped that it might make other people realize that killing themselves is no way to solve problems in life. With time and help, things can always get better.

Junior no longer talks about his suicide attempt. In 1994, his dad told sportswriter Steve Marantz of the *Sporting News*, "We don't worry about it anymore. He was just like any other teenaged kid. We moved on."

BETTER DAYS

The Griffeys did move on to much brighter times during the baseball season in 1988. Junior began the regular season with the San Bernardino Spirit of the Class A California League. He was such a hit in San Bernardino that the team held a "Ken Griffey, Jr. Poster Night" and it was a sellout.

One night in April 1988, Ken, Sr. got his first good look at how well his son was playing. About 2,500 fans were at Fiscalini Field that night to see the Spirit take on a team from Palm Springs. Junior was leading the California League with a .520 batting average, four homers, and 11 RBIs. When he went to bat for the first time, the stadium announcer boomed, "Yes, indeedy, boys and girls, what time is it?"

"It's Griffey time!" roared the fans.

Ken, Sr. shook his head. He couldn't believe what he was seeing and hearing.

He was speechless.

"I just kept saying 'Dad? Dad? Dad?'" Junior says, "He didn't say anything."

As usual, Junior felt nervous with his dad there at the game. Between pitches, he sneaked a peek at Ken, Sr. who was sitting in the stands. With the count at two balls and one strike, Junior bunted the ball down the third–base line. He raced safely to first before the third baseman could make a throw. In the stands, his father grinned.

"I was going to get at least one hit," Junior later told reporters, "even if he gets on me about having to bunt."

In the sixth inning, team officials invited Ken, Sr. to move up to the radio–broadcast booth. When the stadium announcer introduced Ken, Sr. to the crowd, there were loud cheers. Junior was reminded of his dad's presence and struck out in his next at–bat.

In the eighth inning, San Bernadino was ahead, 9–5, when Junior went to bat. He was so desperate to get a good, solid hit that he used his third bat of the game.

With the count at three balls and two strikes, Junior blasted a fastball deep to leftfield. The outfielder ran back, but the ball sailed over the fence. It landed in a clump of trees more than 400 feet from home plate.

In the radio booth, Ken, Sr. put his hand to his mouth and mumbled, "Did you see how far that ball went?"

When Junior crossed home plate, he pointed up at his dad as if to say, "See? How did you like that?"

After 58 games, Junior was batting .338, with 42 RBIs. He led the league with 11 homers and 32 stolen bases. Then he tried to make a diving catch and strained his back. On June 9, he was placed on the disabled list, and he didn't play again until August 15. With the end of the season approaching, the Mariners decided to promote him to their Double A team in Vermont.

Junior did well at the next higher minor league level, even though his back was still so sore he could only play as a designated hitter. In 17 games, he hit .279, with two homers and 10 RBIs.

Junior's fine season showed that he had the talent to rise through the minors quickly. But could he rise quickly enough to make the majors while his dad was still there? Time was running out for Ken, Sr.

RUNNING OUT OF TIME

When spring training began in 1989, there was a good chance that not even one Griffey would play in the major leagues that season. Ken, Sr. had been released by the Braves in July of the year before. In August, he got another shot with the Reds, signing on as a free agent, but he didn't play much during the rest of the 1988 season. He knew he would have to have a very good spring if he wanted to stay on the team.

Before training camp, Ken, Sr. said to his son, "Hurry up and make it [to the majors]. This might be my last season."

Ken, Sr. didn't really expect the two of them to be in the majors together. "It meant pressure on both of us," he said. "I had to be good enough to stick around. He had to be a heck of a player at his young age to get here that quickly."

The Mariners were impressed with Junior's progress, but they thought he needed one more season in the minors. Hopes for a Griffey family reunion on the field of dreams grew dim.

Junior was only three months past his 19th birthday when he reported to the Mariners' training camp, in Arizona. Manager Jim Lefebvre [le-FEE-ver] had heard a lot about him and was eager to see what Junior could do. Junior made the manager's eyes pop out by setting a Mariners' spring–training record by getting at least one hit in 15 straight games.

Junior's hot streak presented the Mariners with a tough decision about where he belonged. On the one hand, the team had never had a winning record since it joined the league in 1977. It needed a star to lift the team and to draw fans. On the other hand, team officials didn't want to rush Junior to the majors. They were worried that his confidence might be hurt or destroyed if he struggled and had to go back to the minors. They were also afraid that Junior might not be able to handle the pressure of being compared to his dad.

"I've seen guys with tremendous talent, but to say he can play day-to-day major league baseball at age nineteen is a heck of a statement," the manager told reporters. "If we rush him, it could set him back a couple of years."

Mr. Lefebvre told Junior to relax and not worry about making the team. Relaxing wasn't easy. Junior had become one of the biggest stories in baseball that spring. Reporters from national magazines and television shows followed him constantly.

Junior wanted very much to make the team. "I'll be upset if I don't make it, but it's up to them and I won't cause problems," he said. "I feel I can play every day right now, even though I know I still have lots to learn. I am a little amazed I've come this far this fast."

He was coming far — and fast. In all, Junior hit .359 in 26 exhibition games. He set Mariner team spring-training records with 33 hits and 21 RBIs. He also played great defense.

MAKING THE TEAM

On March 29, Manager Jim Lefebvre asked Junior to step into his office.

"This is the most difficult decision a manager has to make," Mr. Lefebvre said seriously. He watched Junior's spirits sink. Then Mr. Lefebvre dropped the bomb: "You've made the team," he said. "Congratulations! You're my starting centerfielder."

Junior later told reporters how it felt to hear that great news. "My heart started ticking again," he said. "Those are probably the best words I've ever heard. At least in the top three."

"What are the other two?" a reporter asked.

"[When my parents said] 'You can keep the BMW,' and my parents telling me 'I love you,'" Junior replied.

The next day, Junior got more good news. Ken, Sr. had done his part to fulfill the family dream by batting .333 in his first 21 at-bats that spring and had made the Reds. He had a one-year contract to play for them. The Griffeys were about to become the first father and son to play in the major leagues at the same time.

>> MAKING HISTORY

As the historic Opening Day of the 1989 season approached, Birdie helped Junior set up his new life as a big-leaguer. She drove his car to Seattle, where she found him an apartment and bought him some clothes. The Mariners did not allow players to wear jeans or sneakers on road trips, so Birdie bought Junior a suit, three pairs of dress pants, sweaters, and two pairs of shoes. She also hired an accountant to keep track of Junior's money. Junior would be getting two paychecks every month, and he agreed to send one of them home.

On April 3, Ken, Sr. and the Reds opened the 1989 season in Cincinnati against the Los Angeles Dodgers. Later that day, Junior and the Mariners played the A's in Oakland. Ken, Sr. didn't get a hit, but Junior cracked a double off Dave Stewart in his first official major league at-bat. The hit was extra special because Ken, Sr.'s first career big-league hit had also been a double.

Later that night, Ken, Sr. saw a replay of Junior's hit on television. "I'll tell you the truth, I cried," he says. "They showed me running in my Reds uniform in 1975 and then him in a Mariners uniform."

HANDLING THE PRESSURE

Junior's rookie season had begun well, but the Mariners still had one big question waiting to be answered: How would Junior handle things if he started to struggle?

"The only thing we don't know about him is how he will face that eight-to-nine-game slump," said Mariner outfielder Jeffrey Leonard. "It's going to come, so we have to wait and see how he handles it."

Mariner general manager Woody Woodward agreed. "That's what we're waiting to see," he said. "The guys who are successful adjust to adversity."

Sure enough, Junior failed to get a hit in his next 18 at-bats. But he didn't panic. "I just tried not to worry about anything," he says. "You know what they say: You shouldn't get too high or too low."

As he always did during tough times, Junior kept in touch with his family. He was on the phone every day for up to four hours talking to his dad, mom, brother, and girlfriend, Missy Parrett, whom he knew from Cincinnati.

On April 10, Junior celebrated his dad's 39th birthday by bashing a home run off Eric King of the Chicago White Sox at the Kingdome. It was Junior's first at-bat of the season in front of the Mariners' home fans and he hit the homer with his first swing of the game.

After the game ended, Junior called his dad to say the homer was a birthday present. "You're not getting away that cheap," Ken, Sr. laughed. "Send me a present through the mail."

Ten days later, Ken, Sr. got his first chance to watch Junior in major league action. The Reds weren't playing that day, so he and Birdie traveled from Cincinnati to Comiskey Park in Chicago.

"I'm nervous," Ken, Sr. told reporters. "My palms are sweaty. I never dreamed about this happening. I figured that when he signed with the Mariners, it would take at least four years for him to reach the majors."

"I'm treating this just like a Little League game," Birdie added. "That way, I'm not as nervous as I should be."

Junior was nervous, too. He knew his parents were in the stands. He flied out his first time up, and when he struck out in his second at–bat, he slammed the bat handle on the ground in frustration.

In the seventh inning, Junior finally got a hit. It was a tie–breaking single that sparked the Mariners to a 5–2 victory. After the game, Junior greeted his dad in the locker room with a high–five and asked, "Do I look okay?"

"You're fine," Ken, Sr. replied. "You're always fine when you're hitting."

PLAYER OF THE WEEK

Junior was *very* fine on April 26 at the Kingdome when he staged a performance against the Blue Jays that highlighted all his talent.

In the first inning, Junior blasted a line drive off the rightfield wall to drive in two runs. In the third, he smashed another double into the rightfield corner.

In the fifth, he singled to start a two-run rally by the Mariners that tied the game at 6-6. Then, in the seventh, Junior pounded a pitch over the rightfield wall to put Seattle in front to stay, 7-6.

In all, Junior had four hits, three RBIs, and a stolen base. The hits gave him a streak of eight hits in eight straight at-bats. That tied the team record.

But Junior's hitting was only part of the story on that fabulous night. In the fifth inning, he made a running, over-the-shoulder catch on the warning track. In the eighth inning, Toronto catcher Pat Borders hit the ball to right-centerfield. Junior cut the ball off and held Pat to a single. The play snuffed out Toronto's last chance to rally and tie the game.

"Every time we fought back, there he was," Blue Jay coach John McLaren said after the game. "He's a force to be reckoned with, a force right now."

"I was pretty sure coming in that Griffey was for real," said Fred McGriff, Toronto's slugging first baseman. "He is. He's no fluke."

Jim Lefebvre agreed. "For nine innings tonight, Ken Griffey was the living definition of the word 'impact,'" he said. "What he showed out there tonight is what it's all about, folks."

Junior wasn't impressed with what he had done. "I'm not really jumping up and down inside," he told reporters. "This was nice, fun. But it was only one game and one game does not make a career. I'll be back out here tomorrow trying to make it nine straight hits."

The next night, Junior failed to get that ninth straight hit. But he had put together a streak that included 11 straight times where he reached base safely. The American League honored him as its Player of the Week for April 23 to 27.

A LIKEABLE LITTLE BROTHER

Over in the National League, Ken, Sr. wasn't playing much. The Reds were using him mostly as a pinch–hitter. But one day in early May, he got his first chance to start in a game and belted his first hit of the season. It was a home run. The game was shown live on the message board of the Kingdome while the Mariners were doing their pre–game workout. When Junior saw his dad's homer, he happily high–fived his teammates.

The other Mariners got a kick out of Junior. "He's like a little brother to most of the guys," second baseman Harold Reynolds said.

Junior loved to joke around and play pranks in the clubhouse. He drank soda instead of beer, and listened to rap music on headphones before games. He put an expensive stereo system with 22 speakers in one of his cars. "They make the car vibrate," Junior told a reporter.

And players and fans alike loved the way Ken, Jr. made everything look so easy. Most batters take extra batting practice and study the pitchers they are going to face. It helps them get hits if they know what kind of pitches the pitcher is likely to throw. But Ken, Jr. didn't seem to need that.

One day before the Mariners played the Tigers, a reporter asked Junior if he would play against pitcher Frank Tanana. The reporter wanted to know because Frank was a lefty and Junior had batted only .212 against lefty pitchers in 1988.

"Why wouldn't I play?" Junior asked. "Who's Tanana? Some rookie?" Not quite. Frank Tanana had been a top major league pitcher for 17 years!

"I don't know who's pitching tonight," Junior explained. "I don't even know the schedule. How am I supposed to know who's pitching? I couldn't care less. He's still got to throw me something I can hit. It just adds more pressure to know what a guy throws. You start looking for this or that and all of a sudden he's snuck a 37 mile-per-hour fastball by you." (A 37 mile-per-hour fastball isn't very fast.)

Manager Jim Lefebvre didn't mind Junior's unusual approach to hitting. "He's so far ahead of himself as a young player," he said. "He can hit every pitch. He just goes up there and looks for a ball to hit. It makes no difference to him."

Sometimes the three Mariner outfielders gathered in the outfield while a new pitcher was warming up. Instead of discussing where they should play the next hitter, Junior would talk to his teammates about his favorite songs and rock bands.

"He has so much fun out there that he completely forgets what's going on," Gene Clines, the Mariner batting coach, said.

JUNIOR'S 1989 SEASON

▸ Made the Mariners at age 19 by batting .359 with two homers and 26 RBIs in 26 spring training games.

▸ Became the first son ever to play in the majors while his father was still an active player.

▸ Doubled in his first big-league at-bat.

▸ Homered in his first at-bat in the Kingdome.

▸ Finished with a .264 batting average, 16 homers, 61 RBIs, and 16 stolen bases.

"He's not a student of the game," Ken, Sr. explained. "He plays on instinct and ability, and sometimes very little else. Once he matures a bit — and his mother isn't sure that day ever will come — he'll be a very, very difficult opponent on a baseball field."

BIG HITS, BIG PLAYS

Junior was already a difficult opponent. Against the Milwaukee Brewers at the Kingdome on May 16, he pinch–hit for the first time and blasted the first pitch for a game-winning, two-run homer in the bottom of the ninth. Four days later, he hit a three-run homer against the New York Yankees in the bottom of the seventh to give the Mariners a 6–4 win. The next day, he spoiled Yankee pitcher Clay Parker's shutout with a two-run, inside-the-park homer in the ninth inning.

Junior's defensive plays were breathtaking. In the bottom of the ninth of a tie game at Fenway Park, in Boston, Massachusetts, Red Sox hitting star Wade Boggs hit a ball to deep left-centerfield. The shot looked like a certain triple. Junior dashed after the ball and leaped to catch it just before his back crashed into the padded outfield wall. He fell to the ground for a moment and then lifted his glove to show he had caught the ball. The Red Sox fans gave him a loud round of cheers.

THE PITFALL OF POPULARITY

Junior was playing so well and fans loved his sweet personality so much that in May, the Pacific Trading Cards company introduced the Ken Griffey, Jr. chocolate bar. Each bar had one of 12 different images of Junior in action on it. The company paid Junior $5,000 to let it use his name and he received five cents from every bar that was sold. In one month, Junior earned more than $30,000 from candy sales. "People were screaming for them," says Mike Cramer, the president of the company.

Unfortunately, Junior didn't get to enjoy eating many of his candy bars. He has a mild allergy to chocolate and breaks out in a rash if he eats too much.

Other popular "Junior" items were T-shirts and a poster of Junior and Ken, Sr. posing together in their major league uniforms. Fans bought more than 30,000 copies of the poster during the first two weeks it was on sale. The Mariners held Ken Griffey Poster Night on June 4 and Junior made sure it was extra-special by hitting a game-winning homer.

Junior became so popular that each week he had to refuse about a dozen requests for appearances and product endorsements. Handling so much attention wasn't easy and Junior sometimes did a poor job.

When the Mariners went to Calgary, Alberta, Canada, to play an exhibition game against one of their minor league teams, a small army of Canadian reporters and television crews showed up. Junior was rude to the reporters and he refused to do interviews with the television crews. The next day, a sports columnist for the *Calgary Sun* newspaper wrote that Junior was nothing more than a spoiled brat.

The Mariners were upset with Junior. Team officials told him that his behavior was no way for their biggest star to act. But they also understood that he needed help handling all the demands for his time. The team decided that the way to handle things was to limit his interviews to formal 20-minute press conferences in cities where the team played on road trips.

"We've never had a player receive this kind of attention," Mariner spokesman Ethan Kelly explained to reporters.

"It hasn't gotten out of hand, but it's something that could," Jim Lefebvre said. "We want Junior to stay focused on baseball."

SEATTLE

Seattle is the largest city in the state of Washington. It has a population of about two million people and is located on the eastern shore of Puget Sound, about 125 miles from the Pacific Ocean. Besides being a famous shipping port, it is also the home of the Boeing Aircraft Corporation, the 607-foot tall "Space Needle" observation tower, and the Seattle SuperSonics NBA basketball team.

ACCIDENTS WILL HAPPEN

Unfortunately, Junior did not get the chance to stay focused on baseball for very long. On July 25, he slipped and fell in the shower and broke a bone in the little finger on his left hand. That was very bad news for a lefty hitter. He was batting .287 with 13 homers and 45 RBIs at the time. Many people thought he was a lock to win the American League Rookie of the Year Award.

"It's pretty disappointing," Junior told reporters, "but there's nothing I can do."

Junior's injury was disappointing for the Mariners, too. Ten players, including Jay Buhner, Alvin Davis, and star pitcher Erik Hanson, had been unable to play at one time or another because of injuries that season. The team was in fifth place with a 48–50 record, but it had a shot at its first winning season.

"I'm so dazed right now," Jim Lefebvre said. "We finally start to get healthy and playing well and then, boom, this happens."

Junior was placed on the disabled list and did not play again until August 20. When he returned, he tried too hard to pick up where he had left off and it made him play poorly. He hit only three homers and batted .181 in September and October.

"He was trying to catch up with the other Rookie of the Year candidates with one swing," Jim Lefebvre explained to reporters. "Pretty typical for a nineteen-year-old kid, really. He lost his poise."

Junior agreed. "I was worrying about hitting the ball seven hundred feet," he said. "I just wanted twenty home runs."

Junior finished his rookie season in the majors with 16 homers, 61 RBIs, 16 stolen bases, and a .264 batting average. He also had 12 assists (a fielder is credited with an "assist" when he throws out a runner) and he led all American League outfielders with six double plays. When the Baseball Writers Association voted for the A.L. Rookie of the Year, Junior finished third behind pitchers Gregg Olson of the Orioles and Tom Gordon of the Kansas City Royals.

In his first major league season, Junior had shown brilliant flashes of talent. He was already a rising star who promised to be even better than "The Original Griffey."

>> THE ORIGINAL GRIFFEY

When Junior reached the major leagues in 1989, his dad started calling himself "The Original Griffey." So, how different are The Original Griffey and the Junior version?

"I like to say there's a lot of his dad in him," says Jim Lefebvre. "Junior and Ken Griffey, Senior really are quite a bit alike. He's got great speed just like his dad. He's got a great swing, just like his dad."

As people, though, the two Kens are different. Junior is lighthearted and fun-loving. Ken, Sr. is easy-going and thoughtful, and much more quiet. He doesn't show his emotions as openly as his son does.

Junior's personality is closer to his mom's. Birdie is very talkative, but also strong-willed. She's not shy about making her thoughts and opinions known. Just think about the time she scolded Junior when he was thinking about quitting minor league baseball!

Ken, Jr. and Ken, Sr. have also led quite different lives. Junior grew up in a family that was well-off. He was driven to Little League games in a Rolls Royce. Ken, Sr. never had it that easy when he was a kid.

Ken Griffey, Sr. was born on April 10, 1950 in Donora, Pennsylvania. He was one of six kids. His family lived in a housing project. Life became very hard when his father, Buddy, abandoned the family. Ken was two years old at the time. His mom, Ruth, took odd jobs and went on welfare to put food on the table.

Ken didn't see his dad again for five years. When Buddy showed up at the family's apartment one day, Ken didn't recognize him and began to close the door in his face! Buddy later moved to Cleveland and Ken did not see him again until the 1975 World Series. They never became close.

TOUGH TIMES *AND* TRUE LOVE

When Ken was a kid and wanted to play baseball, he had to walk five miles to the field. His worn-out shoes were often patched with cardboard. As a teenager, he had to work to help out his family. Among the jobs he had were working in a grocery store, building bombs for the Vietnam War in a steel factory, and reading electric meters at people's houses for the local power company. The meter-reading job turned out to be dangerous. "I had bad experiences with dogs," he says. "I'd carry six cans of dog mace around with me when I was reading meters." Ken, Sr.'s first car was a 1965 Plymouth that cost $435 and stalled out when he stopped at red lights. Junior's first car was a $30,000 BMW.

Ken, Sr. loved sports. Like Junior, he starred in more than one sport in high school. He won all-state honors as an end on the football team and he also ran track.

"I played basketball, football, and baseball, but baseball was the only sport in which I thought I could make it professionally," he says.

Ken was a top jock at Donora High and very popular. One of his admirers was a girl named Alberta Littleton, who was called "Birdie."

Birdie had six brothers and sisters. Her dad worked as a crane operator in a steel mill and her mom was a nurse's aide. Birdie was very athletic. She played basketball and volleyball.

Birdie's best friend wanted to take Ken to the Sadie Hawkins Day dance at the high school. (At a Sadie Hawkins dance, the girls invite the boys.) When her friend couldn't find the courage to ask Ken, she asked Birdie to do it after class one day.

"Will you go with her?" Birdie asked Ken.

"No," he replied.

"Then will you go with me?" she asked.

"Yes," he said.

Birdie's friend never spoke to her again!

Ken and Birdie went to the dance and starting dating. They were married shortly after they graduated from Donora High.

At that time, Ken's future as a major league ballplayer was hardly certain. He did not have the kind of confidence in his ability that his son later had when he was in high school. When one of Ken's friends told Ken he wasn't good enough to make the local American Legion baseball team, he didn't even try out!

HARD WORK PAYS OFF

The following summer, Ken decided to attend a Reds tryout camp in Fayette City, Ohio. He did well and in June 1969, he was drafted by Cincinnati — in the 29th round. Ken was given an athletic supporter, a Reds warmup jacket, and a pair of white socks. That's all. When Junior was drafted by the Mariners in the first round, he got a $160,000 bonus just to sign his contract.

Ken, Sr. began his pro career with Bradenton of the Gulf Coast League, which was for rookies. Within six months, Ken, Jr. was born. His father was only 19 at the time — the same age Junior was when he made it to the major leagues.

Ken, Sr. spent almost five years in the minors. He was one of three promising young outfielders in the Reds minor league system. The other two, George Foster and Ed Armbrister, later became his teammates in Cincinnati.

The Reds saw that Ken had the talent to be a good major league player some day. They especially liked how fast he could run. Jim Snyder, Ken's manager at Three Rivers, told reporters, "Ken has everything he needs to become a big-league star. His speed is unbelievable and things just seem to happen when he's in the game."

Unlike Junior, who rose to the majors mostly on natural talent, Ken, Sr. worked hard and learned from other players. Reds' stars Joe Morgan and Bobby Tolan taught him how to get a better head start when stealing bases by "reading" a pitcher's pickoff move. Joe, who became a Hall of Fame second baseman, stole 689 bases during his big-league career. Bobby, a speedy outfielder, led the National League with 57 steals in 1970.

In 1973, Ken batted .327 at Indianapolis in the Triple A American Association and was promoted to the Reds during the last month of the season. He hit .384 with 33 hits in 86 at-bats during his first taste of major league action. When he slumped in the early part of the 1974 season, he was sent back to the minors. But he came back to the Reds to stay a few months later.

THE BIG RED MACHINE

Ken was a very good player on a great team, known as the Big Red Machine. This team won the World Series in 1975 and 1976, and the National League West Division title in 1979. Ken batted .300 or higher four times in his first five full seasons with the Reds and almost won the 1976 National League batting championship. He hit .336 that season, but was beaten out on the final day of the season by Bill Madlock of the Pirates, who finished with a .339 average.

FATHER AND SON

Many fathers and sons have played in the major leagues. Here are some of the most famous:

The Alomars: Sandy, Sr. played infield for six different teams between 1964 and 1978. One son, second baseman Roberto, played on the same teams with another son, Sandy, Jr., a catcher two different times. In 1988 and 1989, they both played on the San Diego Padres. In 1999 and 2000, the brothers both played on the Cleveland Indians. Both have been all-stars.

The Alous: Felipe and his brothers Matty and Jesus were star outfielders during the 1960s and 1970s. All three were teammates on the San Francisco Giants in 1963. Felipe's son Moises played his first full season in the majors with the Montreal Expos in 1992. That was also the first year Felipe served as the Expos' manager.

Ken combined his fine hitting with excellent base–running speed. He stole 102 bases in his first five seasons and also beat out 156 infield hits.

"They said I introduced a new statistic into baseball: the infield hit," Ken says. "Not the bunt, but the ground ball you beat out."

▶ ANOTHER FATHER AND SON

The Bonds: Bobby was a fast, powerful outfielder for eight different teams between 1968 and 1981. He set a major league record by hitting 30 or more homers and stealing 30 or more bases in a season five times. Barry is a National League All-Star and four-time MVP. In 1996, he became the first N.L. player to hit 40 or more homers and steal 40 or more bases in the same season. In 2001, he set the all-time single-season home-run record with 73.

Ken, Sr. never had as much power as Junior does. He hit only 40 homers total during his first five full seasons. (In 1997 and 1998, Junior hit 56!) The most notable homer Ken, Sr. ever hit was in the 1980 All-Star Game, and it contributed to his being named the game's Most Valuable Player.

A QUIET STAR

Unlike his son, Ken, Sr. was never a big, popular star. He was quiet and dependable. Famous Reds such as Pete Rose, Johnny Bench, Tony Perez, Joe Morgan, and George Foster always overshadowed him. Reds manager Sparky Anderson summed up what Ken was all about when he said, "Just pencil his name in the lineup and forget about him."

"If I was a scout, what would I report about Ken Griffey?" Ken, Sr. once was asked. "Very easy–going, likes to take things in stride, very quiet, even subdued."

Ken's subdued personality was quite a contrast to that of more colorful major leaguers. And once, he was even expected to fill the shoes of one of the most colorful of all: Reggie Jackson of the New York Yankees. Ken, Sr. was traded to the Yankees before the 1982 season, after Reggie Jackson had left New York as a free agent to join the California Angels. Ken was to take Reggie's place as the team's rightfielder. Reggie was a slugger known as "Mr. October" for his heroics in the playoffs and World Series. He was as colorful as Ken was quiet.

"I can't do what Reggie does," Ken told reporters after he was traded. "My job is getting on base, stealing bases, scoring runs. Production. Whatever it takes to win a game, I'm supposed to do."

Ken's four–and–a–half seasons in New York were often frustrating. He had injured his knee in 1978 and had needed surgery. The injury continued to bother him when he was with the Yankees. He was switched to first base in his second season there. It was easier on his legs.

The highlight of Ken's time with the Yankees came in 1985 against the Red Sox at Yankee Stadium. The Yankees were leading, 6–5, in the top of the ninth when Boston second baseman Marty Barrett hit a long drive to leftfield. Ken raced back, jumped, and climbed the wall. He was more than 10 feet off the ground when he caught the ball. Then he fell back to the ground and did a backward somersault. The crowd went wild and the catch saved the win for the Yankees.

When Junior went to Yankee Stadium for the first time as a Mariner in 1989, he went to the spot where his dad had made that spectacular catch. "I studied the angle he had and tried to figure out how high he went," he says. "I rated him a ten on the catch and a two on the dismount."

Ken, Sr. was traded to the Braves in June of 1986. As he got older and began to lose some of his skills, he remained a valuable player because of his quiet leadership and experience.

STACKING UP

Naturally, the two Ken Griffeys have been asked many times to compare themselves to each other. "There's nothing to compare," Ken, Sr. says, "He's bigger (Junior is 6 feet 3 inches; Ken, Sr. is 6 feet), stronger, and capable of doing more things than I ever could." What would you expect a proud father to say?

Junior disagrees. "We do everything alike, except I hit more home runs," he says.

"I'm not a home-run hitter," Ken, Sr. said in 1982. "I'm glad I recognized that for myself when I first started playing minor league baseball. When you try to be something you're not, you only mess things up. The thing I demand from myself more than anything else is consistency. I try to hit the ball the same way all the time and drive it between the outfielders if I can."

Ken, Sr.'s whole approach to hitting is very different from Junior's. Ken, Sr. always looked for a fastball and tried to adjust to other pitches. "The best pitch in baseball, when it's thrown properly, is the fastball," he says, "because it can overpower the hitter. So you have to be ready for it and if you're me, you never guess."

Junior doesn't guess, either. He doesn't even think about what kind of pitch is being thrown.

Ken, Sr. admits that Junior has a better throwing arm and just as much speed. Yet, Ken, Sr. has stolen 20 or more bases in a season three times, and through 2001, Junior had done it only twice. Ken, Sr. also played in three playoffs and two World Series. Junior has made it to the playoffs twice with the Mariners, but never to the Series. He would like to.

"He doesn't like to lose," Ken, Sr. says. "He gets that from both parents." That sounds like a good way to produce a winner, doesn't it?

FATHER-SON REUNION

In his first major league season, Junior had shown brilliant flashes of talent. During the winter of 1989–90, he grew one-and-a-half inches and gained 15 pounds, so he was 6 feet 3 inches and 195 pounds. Bigger and stronger, he got off to a roaring start the next season.

Junior was named the American League Player of the Month for April. He had hit .388, with five homers and 17 RBIs. By the middle of May, he was leading the league in hitting with a .370 average. He also became the first Mariner ever selected by fans across the country to start in an All-Star Game.

While Junior was in Chicago for the All-Star Game at Wrigley Field, in July, he was asked by a reporter to name the accomplishment that made him most proud.

"It's being in the big leagues and still having my dad here," Junior replied. "That means the most to me."

Little did Junior know that seven weeks later, having his dad "here" would mean "with the Mariners."

Things had not been going well for Ken, Sr. in Cincinnati. He had barely played at all after July 4

and hit only .206, with one homer and eight RBIs. On August 18th, the Reds asked him to go on the disabled list even though he wasn't injured. The Reds wanted Ken, Sr. to move in order to make a spot on the roster for another player.

Ken, Sr. decided to retire instead. He figured that he had had a good, long career. He also wanted to be the one who decided when it was time for him to quit. However, someone else had a better idea.

TOGETHER AT LAST

On August 29, 1990, Ken, Sr. was signed by the Mariners. He and Junior were now the first father and son ever to be active players for the same major league team. Ken, Sr. called it the best day of his career.

Junior told reporters that he had been pestering the team for two months about trading for his dad. "I didn't ask for him," he said. "It was more of a demand. I just told dad to get over here. I wanted him around."

Ken, Sr. needed a couple of days to get ready for his first game with Seattle. On August 30, the day before he would actually play, the media started arriving at the Kingdome in huge numbers.

The excitement was building for the Griffeys, too. The afternoon before the game, Junior spent time with his agent, Brian Goldberg. "It's really going to be weird tonight, playing with my dad," Junior said to Brian.

Two hours later, Brian drove Ken, Sr. to the Kingdome. "You know," Ken, Sr. said. "It's going to be weird tonight, playing with my son."

Finally, the big moment arrived. As the Griffeys trotted out to their positions in the outfield, Junior gave his dad a quick wave that could have been a salute.

"I didn't know what to expect," Ken, Sr. says. "It was the most nerve-racking night I've ever spent in my life. I've always had butterflies, but it took a lot more con-centration than I could have imagined."

The situation made Ken, Sr. so shaky before he went to bat, he had to steady himself by holding on to the bat rack in the dugout. "Then I go to the plate and I heard, 'Come on, Dad!'" he says. "That really shook me up. After the first pitch, I settled down."

Royals pitcher Storm Davis threw a fastball, and Ken, Sr. swung and singled to centerfield. Junior followed with a single of his own and the Griffeys were off and running. Ken, Sr. later made a great defensive play, and the happy night was capped off by a 5–2 win.

"Like any other father, I was nervous because I wanted him to do well," Ken, Sr. told reporters after the game. "I know he was just as excited as me."

"I didn't know what to think," Junior said. "I wanted to cry. I just stood there and looked at him in leftfield."

A week later, against Boston, Ken, Sr. hit his first homer as a Mariner. Junior was waiting at the plate to greet him.

Playing with Junior seemed to make Ken, Sr. young again. He was named the American League Player of the Week, batting .632, with one home run and seven RBIs. It was the first time in his 18–year career he had been named Player of the Week.

A SPECIAL MOMENT

One of the most special moments of the season took place on September 14 at Anaheim Stadium. In the first inning, Ken, Sr. blasted a shot to centerfield off Angel pitcher Kirk McCaskill. Home run! When Ken, Sr. crossed home plate, he high–fived Junior and said, "That's the way you do it, son."

JUNIOR'S 1990 SEASON

▷ Became the first son ever to play with his father on the same major league team.

▷ Became the first Mariner ever selected by fans to start in an All-Star Game.

▷ Batted .300 for the first time and also led the Mariners in homers (22) and RBIs (80).

▷ Won his first Gold Glove Award.

Junior followed his dad's example by bashing a home run of his own.

Junior and his dad had a blast being teammates. Junior called his dad "Pops" and loved to walk past his locker and make a wisecrack or ask for money. When he did, Ken, Sr. jokingly threatened to spank him or tell mom.

In all, the Griffeys played together in 15 games that season, winning seven and losing eight. Junior hit .312, with three homers and 11 RBIs in those games. Ken, Sr. topped him by batting .400, with three homers and 16 RBIs.

"That was the best month I've had in the majors," Junior says. "We were having such a great time playing together, being teammates, playing baseball."

Ken, Sr. said, "This is something to cherish."

Junior had some feats of his own to cherish. He had made his first All–Star team and won his first Gold Glove award. His final stats (.300 batting average, 22 homers, 80 RBIs) showed the promise of great things to come.

"He can be as good as he wants to be," said Ken, Sr..

How good did Junior want to be? That was a question he was forced to ask himself during his next season.

>> THE WAKE-UP CALL

The 1991 season began with signs of trouble for the Griffeys. On March 2, Ken, Sr. hurt his neck in a car accident in Phoenix, Arizona. It would keep him from playing regularly. Then the Mariners got off to a terrible start by losing their first six games of the season. They won their next eight, then lost five more in a row.

Losing games began to affect Junior. He hit only two homers and had just seven RBIs during the month of April. "I was down on myself," he says. "I wanted to win so bad, and when we didn't, it was like, 'Oh, no, not again.'" The Mariners were still the only team in the major leagues that had never had a winning season. A lot was expected of them that season. They had young, talented players such as outfielder Jay Buhner and pitcher Randy Johnson. Junior was supposed to lead the way, but he, and the team, struggled.

The season became a roller–coaster ride. The Mariners won 13 of their first 17 games in May. Junior perked up, too, and hit .300, with four homers and 15 RBIs

during the month. But by June 1, there was more bad news. Ken, Sr.'s neck was hurting so much he had to go on the disabled list.

HARD TO RELAX

Junior struggled without his dad around. He hit only .226 during June. Second baseman Harold Reynolds noticed how tense Junior was becoming. One day, when the Mariners were on the road, Harold sat down next to Junior in the dugout during batting practice.

"Why are you putting so much pressure on yourself?" Harold asked him. "Just relax and have fun, and it'll happen."

It was hard for Junior to relax or have fun. By the All-Star break, in July, the Mariners were in sixth place in their division with a 40–42 record.

Junior was hearing a lot of criticism. Sportswriters, and even some major leaguers, were accusing him of not playing as hard as he could.

Junior had heard that criticism before. Early in the 1990 season, Tiger manager Sparky Anderson had scolded him for not running hard to first base after hitting a ground ball. "You're lucky your dad didn't see you when you weren't hustling," Sparky had told him. "People pay money to see you play."

When Junior went to Toronto to play in the 1991 All-Star Game, sportswriter Steve Kelley wrote an open letter to him that was printed in the *Seattle Times* newspaper. It pointed out that Junior had hit only .280, with nine homers, 36 RBIs, and 46 strikeouts during the first half of the season. Those stats were not very good for a player many people thought of as the next Willie Mays.

"We have great expectations for you," Steve wrote. "But now we're beginning to wonder. We don't see the work habits of Willie Mays. We don't see the hunger that drove Mays into the Hall of Fame."

The letter also noted that Junior had been goofing off in batting practice, letting his mind wander during games, making mistakes like not throwing to the cutoff man, and barely running out grounders and fly balls.

"We wonder what a player would be like with your talent and your father's hunger," the columnist wrote. "Ken Griffey, Senior runs harder to first base than you do. Willie Mays was a marvelously talented athlete, but he also worked incredibly hard. It seems as if you are just getting by with just your talent."

Steve added that Junior's contract guaranteed him a huge raise in salary — more than a million dollars — no matter how well he played. "Will you settle for being a multimillionaire instead of a Hall of Famer?" Steve asked. "Maybe now it's time to go to work. Time to be more than just a good player. Time to be great. But some of us wonder if you want it enough."

When Junior read Steve Kelley's letter, an alarm clock went off in his head. "The article made me think about what I was doing," he says.

Junior called Steve to talk about the article and later told reporters, "My intensity is always there, but maybe it doesn't always show. I want to be the best I can be."

SECOND-HALF HEROICS

Junior backed up his words by playing better than ever during the second half of the season. On July 23 at Yankee Stadium, he blasted his first career grand slam to power the Mariners to a 6–1 win. A week later, against the Orioles, he made a great running catch of a 405-foot drive, hit by Randy Milligan with the bases loaded. Then he went to bat in the bottom half of the inning and smacked another grand slam. The Mariners won, 8–2.

In July, Junior led the league in batting with a .434 average, hit five homers, and drove in 25 runs. Meanwhile, the Mariners boosted their record to 54–48.

"Since that article was written, he's done a lot of great things," manager Jim Lefebvre said. "It set him on fire."

By August 16, the Mariners had 10 more wins than losses for the first time in their history. They were in fourth place, only five-and-a-half games behind the first-place Twins. Junior was honored as the American League Player of the Week for batting .542, with three homers and nine RBIs.

"We knew he could do it all," Jim Lefebvre said. "Now he's doing it when it's never counted more."

For the first time in his big–league career, Junior was enjoying the excitement of winning and being in a pennant race. "It's a lot of fun," he told reporters. "This team is great. Everybody knows we're good and that if we play good, fundamental baseball, we can match up with every team."

Junior also downplayed his own accomplishments. "I'm not looking at my numbers," he said. "If you hit .200 and you win, or .300 and you win, it's all the same. Just so you win."

JUNIOR'S 1991 SEASON

- Batted .327 and drove in 100 runs for the first time.
- Hit 22 homers, including the first three grand slams of his career.
- Received more All-Star votes from fans (2,248,396) than any other American League player.
- Won his second Gold Glove award.
- Named the American League's best defensive outfielder by major league managers.

END-OF-SEASON BLUES

Unfortunately for the Mariners, the winning didn't continue. On August 20, they went to Minnesota for a big three-game showdown with the Twins. Seattle was six-and-a-half games behind Minnesota — and lost all three games. Then the Mariners were swept by the Tigers in their *next* three games, in Detroit. Suddenly the Mariners were ten-and-a-half games out of first. Their season was all but over.

Sadly, Ken, Sr.'s season was over, too. He had gone to bat only 85 times all season. On August 31, he announced that he was going to have surgery on his neck. "I can't go any further without pain," he said. "It interferes with my hitting."

Ken, Sr. was expected to be in the hospital for three days, and doctors had told him he could not be physically active for about three months. It was likely that his career was over.

Even though the season ended on a sour note, Junior and his teammates had some things to be proud of. The Mariners finished the 1991 season with an 83–79 record — their first winning record ever. Junior's performance in the second half of the season (.372, 13 homers, 64 RBIs) had been the best of any player in the American League. His final stats included 22 homers, 100 RBIs, and team records for batting average (.327) and doubles (42). He also won his second Gold Glove.

Then Junior had to adjust to some important changes. In November, his dad announced his retirement after 19 seasons in the major leagues. The most surprising change came when the Mariners fired manager Jim Lefebvre. It was a strange move. Jim had just done something no one had ever done before. He had led the Mariners to a winning season. He was replaced by Bill Plummer, starting with the 1992 season.

SHINING IN TOUGH TIMES

And what a disaster that season was. In 1992, the Mariners suffered a series of injuries to their best players and sank like a leaky boat. Even Junior got hurt. He sprained his right wrist while diving for a fly ball and went on the disabled list from June 9 to June 25. Seattle had a winning record for only one day that season (it was 10–9 on April 24). The team ended up last in its division, with a final record of 64–98. Bill Plummer was fired at the end of the season and Lou Piniella was chosen to be the team's new manager.

Lost in the shipwreck of the Mariners' season was another fine performance by Junior. He batted .308, reached new career-highs in homers (27) and RBIs (103), and won another Gold Glove.

The highlight of Junior's season came at the All-Star Game, in San Diego. He put another few pages in his family's history book that night.

JUNIOR'S 1992 SEASON

- Set Mariners single-season team records by batting .327 and hitting 42 doubles.
- Became first Mariner ever to have 100 or more RBIs two seasons in a row.
- Became the first son ever to equal his dad's feat of hitting a home run in the All-Star Game and being chosen the game's MVP.
- Won his third straight Gold Glove award.

There were four sons of big leaguers in the American League lineup that night. The starting shortstop was Cal Ripken, Jr. of the Baltimore Orioles. His dad had managed the Orioles from 1987 to April 1988. Sandy Alomar, Jr. whose father had played various infield positions for different teams from 1964 to 1978, started at catcher. Sandy, Jr.'s brother Roberto started at second base. Junior played centerfield, of course, and shined brighter than all the other sons.

In the first inning, Junior singled in a run. In the third inning, he belted a screaming drive over the leftfield fence. The home run made the Griffeys the first father and son both to hit All–Star Game home runs. (Ken, Sr. hit one in 1980, 12 years earlier.)

In the sixth inning, Junior cracked a double to start a four-run rally. The American League won, 13–6. Junior was chosen the game's Most Valuable Player. He and his dad were now the first father and son to win the award.

"He's a very talented kid," said Tom Kelly of the Twins, who managed the American League team. "He's going to be a big-numbers kind of guy."

Tom Kelly was right. In 1993, Junior became a big-numbers guy — especially in the home run department.

BOMBS AWAY

After three full seasons in the majors, Junior had established himself as a mighty power hitter. In 1992, Mariner outfielder Kevin Mitchell told reporters, "I've seen the man on the bench, in a tie game, say to me, 'Do you want me to hit a home run?' Then he does it."

In 1993, Junior did it more than ever.

His first home run of the season came in his first at-bat on Opening Day in the Kingdome. After the first two months of the season, Junior had 10 homers and 30 RBIs. Pitchers became afraid to throw to him so they walked him on purpose. He ended up setting a team record by being walked intentionally 25 times that season.

On June 20th, Junior began a streak of four straight games in which he hit a home run. By the All-Star break, in July, he had hit 22. Of course, he was again elected to the All-Star team.

The day before the All-Star Game at Camden Yards, in Baltimore, Junior treated the fans to an awesome display of power. He competed in a home-run-hitting

contest with several other All-Stars, including slugging outfielder Juan Gonzalez of the Texas Rangers. Each player tried to hit as many home runs as he could before failing to clear the fence 10 times.

Juan got the crowd buzzing by bombing a 473-foot drive off the upper deck in leftfield. He followed it by blasting a 455-foot shot off the wall behind the centerfield fence. No player had ever hit a ball there before, but Junior was not going to be outdone.

During his turn at bat, Junior launched a drive way over the rightfield fence. The ball carried until it hit the wall of a warehouse. The blast was estimated at 445 feet and it made Junior the first player ever to hit a ball off the building.

"I didn't think it was going to get there," he later told reporters. "I was trying to concentrate on the next pitch, then everybody started clapping."

A RUN FOR THE RECORD

Baseball fans really started clapping on July 20 when Junior began a run at one of baseball's most amazing records. In the eighth inning of a game at Yankee Stadium, Junior hit a home run. The next day, he hit another homer, off Yankee pitcher Jimmy Key, in the sixth inning.

The Mariners then traveled to Cleveland to play the Indians. Junior smacked a homer in the first game. That gave him three home runs in three straight games. Something special was happening.

Junior kept hitting home runs. On July 27, in Seattle, Junior blasted a 441-foot grand slam against the Twins.

It was his seventh homer in seven straight games. Junior was now one homer away from tying the major league record, set by Dale Long of the Pirates, in 1956, and tied by Don Mattingly of the Yankees, in 1987.

Don was watching Junior's streak with a lot of interest. He had been a teammate of Ken, Sr.'s on the Yankees from 1982 to 1986. "It's kind of funny that this kid I watched shag fly balls and saw grow up has the chance to tie it or possibly break the record," Don told reporters. "It doesn't bother me at all. It's kind of cool."

On July 28 at the Kingdome, Junior took his shot at tying the record. He struck out in the first inning and grounded out in the fourth. But on his third at-bat in the seventh inning, he smashed the first pitch from Willie Banks of the Twins. The ball sailed high, far, and deep to rightfield. Junior grinned and watched as the ball bounced off the front of the third deck. Home run!

Junior happily bounded around the bases and was given a three-minute standing ovation by the crowd. He came out of the dugout twice to wave to the cheering fans, who gave him another ovation when he trotted out to his position at the end of the inning.

Could Junior break the record? Mariners first baseman Tino Martinez thought so. Tino told reporters, "He's playing way above everybody else in baseball right now."

On July 29, the eyes of the baseball world were on Seattle when the Mariners took on the Twins. A crowd of 45,607 fans showed up at the Kingdome and cheered Junior's every move.

In his first three at-bats, he hit a scorching single and a hard double, but time began to run out. In the seventh inning, Twins relief pitcher Larry Casian threw Junior a perfect pitch to hit for a home run. To everyone's surprise, Junior popped it up. He was out, and he didn't get to bat again. The streak was over.

Junior's streak was truly amazing. It's hard enough for players to get a hit in eight games in a row, let alone eight home runs. The streak gave Junior 30 home runs for the season. That total was another career-high, and he still had two months left in the season.

WIZARD WITH THE GLOVE

Junior's spectacular hitting overshadowed another of his great accomplishments that season. When he made an error on August 8 against Texas, few people realized it was the first one he had made since April 16, 1992. That was 240 games before! He had set a major league record for outfielders by handling 573 "chances" (fielding grounders and flies or making a throw) without an error.

On September 1, Junior hit his 40th homer of the season against the Tigers. He was the first Mariner ever to reach that total in one season.

How was he doing it? Where were all these home runs coming from?

"I don't consider myself a home-run hitter," Junior told a reporter from *Sports Illustrated.* "But when I'm hitting the ball hard, it will go out of the park. During the streak, I didn't do anything differently than anyone else was doing. I just went up there and hit. And hit."

Junior finished the 1993 season with an amazing 45 home runs. He also batted .309, with 109 RBIs, and won his fourth Gold Glove. The 109 RBIs made him only the fourth player in big-league history to have 100 or more RBIs in a season three seasons in a row before reaching the age of 24.

There was no question that 1993 had been Junior's best season yet. It didn't seem possible that he could do much better than he had done that season, but he was just getting warmed up. The 1994 season would be a real blast.

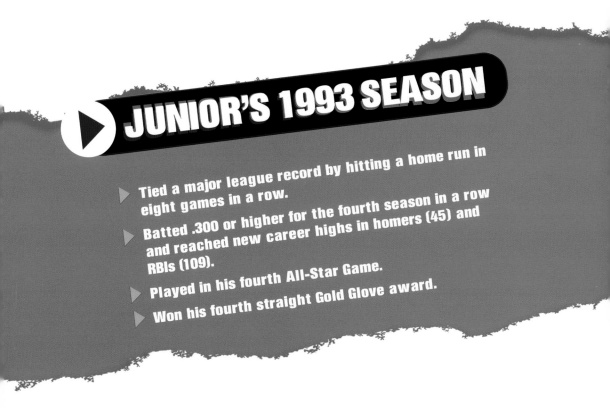

JUNIOR'S 1993 SEASON

▶ Tied a major league record by hitting a home run in eight games in a row.

▶ Batted .300 or higher for the fourth season in a row and reached new career highs in homers (45) and RBIs (109).

▶ Played in his fourth All-Star Game.

▶ Won his fourth straight Gold Glove award.

>> THE ROOF FALLS IN

The year 1994 began with great joy for Junior. His wife, Melissa, whom he had married in 1992, gave birth to a son on January 19. Junior and Melissa talked about what to name their baby. The obvious choice was George Kenneth Griffey, III. But that seemed too formal, so they chose Trey Kenneth instead. The word "trey" [tray] means "three."

Junior instantly fell in love with his baby. Ken, Sr., who was now a proud grandfather, noticed that being a father made Junior more responsible at home and even happier at the ballpark.

"He has changed a lot since he's become an old man," Ken, Sr. said. "He doesn't want to be called Kid anymore."

When spring training began, Junior showed increased hustle and determination. He started to study the game more closely. He watched videotapes of his at-bats to see when he was swinging properly and when he was making mistakes.

It was clear that Junior was preparing himself for a monster season. A lot was expected of the Mariners.

Major League Baseball had reorganized its leagues. Each league had three divisions, instead of two. Seattle was in the American League West with the Oakland A's, California Angels, and Texas Rangers. The Mariners had more than enough talent to finish ahead of those teams.

ON FIRE

After the regular season opened, on April 4, home runs started flying out of ballparks in record numbers. Junior hit eight homers in April. Then he roared through May, during which he had a streak of eight in ten games. By May 30, he had hit 22 dingers. That set a major league record for most homers during the first two months of a season. The previous record of 20 had been set by Hall of Famer Mickey Mantle, in 1956.

Junior was on a pace to hit 74 homers in the season. That would break the single-season record of 61, set by Roger Maris of the Yankees in 1961.

Despite Junior's performance, the Mariners were having a hard time winning. They lost the first five games of the season. But because their division was weak, they wound up in first place at the end of April, with an 11–13 record. Then came a disastrous slump.

The Mariners went to Oakland on May 23 and lost two out of three games to a team with a 4–27 record. The next stop was Milwaukee. There Seattle was swept in three games by the Brewers, who had lost 14 in a row.

Junior became so frustrated he told a reporter from the *News Tribune* of Tacoma, "It takes heart to win and we don't have enough here to win the division. It's easier to roll over and quit. People say we've never won here and never will. For some players, it's easier to let it keep happening than try to change it."

Junior even threatened to leave the Mariners when his contract ended after the 1996 season. "I love Seattle," he said, "but losing is killing me."

Junior's anger lit a fire under his teammates. They went out the next day and thrashed the Twins, 12–0.

"I told Junior that I was happy to hear what he said," manager Lou Piniella said after the game. "It was the

JUNIOR'S 1994 SEASON

- Broke Mickey Mantle's major league record for most home runs during the first two months of the season by hitting 22.
- Received more All-Star votes (6,079,688) than any player ever.
- Won the Home Run Derby at the All-Star Game by blasting seven, including one that traveled 512 feet!
- At age 24, became the youngest player ever to have started in five All-Star Games.

same theme I've tried to get across for a while, but sometimes players listen better to another player. Every player should be tired of losing. You play every day, and it's a grind. The more you win, the more fun you have. All the young man was saying is that he's tired of losing."

THE BLASTS KEEP COMING

During the next month, Junior took out his anger on the baseball itself. On June 24, in the Kingdome, he blasted a 400-foot shot off pitcher Paul Assenmacher of the White Sox. It was Junior's 32nd homer as well as his 23rd 400-foot blast of the season.

"He said he was going to go deep," White Sox first baseman Frank Thomas told reporters after the game. "I could see it in his eyes, and he's definitely in a groove."

Frank was in a groove, too. During that weekend series in Seattle, he and Junior found themselves locked in a home run duel. Frank had hit 28; Junior 32. *Both* players were on pace to break Roger Maris's single-season record.

Would they do it? Since 1961, no one had come within eight homers of 61. In 1987, Eric Davis of the Reds set a National League record by hitting 19 homers before June 1 and finished the season with 37. In 1989, Kevin Mitchell of the San Francisco Giants hit 31 before the All-Star break in July, but just 16 more after that.

Junior didn't think he had much of a chance. "I'm still not a power hitter," he insisted. "Power hitters think about one thing when they step up to the plate, and that's hitting the ball out of the ballpark. I'm not thinking home run."

BIG-LEAGUE ATTENTION

However, the public and the media were thinking about home runs. The attention on Junior and Frank increased. People wondered if the two sluggers could handle the distractions and pressure. When Roger Maris was trying to break Babe Ruth's record of 60 homers in a season, the pressure became so intense that his hair began to fall out.

Not to worry. The morning before the Mariners and White Sox would wrap up their three–game series, Junior hung out with Frank for a while. "We didn't talk about baseball," Junior told reporters. "We did check each other's hair, though. 'Yours falling out?' 'Naw, yours?'"

The two stars spent most of their time talking about their kids. "You talk about the pressure of hitting home runs," Junior laughed. "I'd rather go and try to hit a home run than change my son's diaper any day. I get one leg down, the other one goes up. I get both legs down and all of a sudden, he's sitting up."

In addition to the pressure, there was the looming possibility of a baseball strike. The team owners and players were locked in a nasty dispute about salaries. The owners wanted a "salary cap," or limit, on the amount of money each team could pay to all its players. The players insisted they would never agree to that.

Junior was asked if he was worried about a strike ruining his chance for the record. "I'm not even thinking about it," he said, referring to the record. "If it happens, it happens. If it doesn't, it wasn't meant to be."

On June 22, Junior hit his 31st homer of the season in a 12–3 win over the Angels in Anaheim. His shot broke Babe Ruth's record, set in 1928, of 30 homers by the end of June.

THE RACE HEATS UP

The great home run chase continued into July. By the All-Star break, Junior was tied with Matt Williams of the Giants for the major league lead in homers. Each had 33. Frank Thomas was right behind with 32.

Of all the great performers that season, Junior was given the biggest salute by the fans. He received a record total of 6,079,688 All-Star votes. That was almost *two million* more than the record set by Rod Carew in 1977.

Junior showed what he was about at the All-Star home-run-hitting contest on July 11. *Sports Illustrated For Kids* magazine sent two reporters to Three Rivers Stadium, in Pittsburgh, Pennsylvania. They sat in the open press box above the rightfield wall. Junior had them flinching and ducking for cover as he blasted shot after shot at them and over them.

In all, Junior put four blasts into the upper deck in rightfield. One of them traveled 512 feet! "I can't hit the ball harder than that," he said later.

Frank Thomas ended up hitting the longest shot that afternoon: a 519-foot drive off the face of the upper deck in left-centerfield. But Junior won the contest with a total of seven homers.

The Mariners opened the second half of the season in Seattle against the Yankees and were sunk when New York swept all four games. Two days later, the roof fell in, literally.

On July 19, tiles attached to the ceiling of the Kingdome started to fall into the stands. The Kingdome was found to be so unsafe it had to be closed. The Mariners were forced to play their next 20 games on the road. Still, they won the last six of those 20, going 11 and nine. They climbed into third place, just two games behind first-place Texas.

ON STRIKE

Then on August 12, the Mariners' and Junior's momentum all came to an abrupt halt. The major league baseball players went on strike. When the players and the owners couldn't resolve their differences, the season was cancelled for good on September 14. For the first time in 90 years, there would be no playoffs and no World Series. And no one would know whether anyone could have broken the home run record. Matt Williams finished with 43 homers, Junior 40, and Frank Thomas 38.

Junior went home to play with Trey and spend more time with Melissa. "I'm on baby-sitting patrol," he told a reporter from Newsday. "I'm really frustrated because it was a good year for baseball to break through, as far as the records changing. Everyone wanted to see what was going to happen. Everyone wanted the whole year."

Junior summed up the 1994 season best when he said, "We picked a bad year to have a good year."

BACK IN THE SWING

No one knew what was going to happen with the 1995 baseball season. The players' strike that had begun in August the year before continued into spring training. Team owners tried to put together "replacement" teams made up of minor league players and former major leaguers, but few fans were interested in watching them. The big dispute was finally settled in court.

On April 2, a judge ruled that the owners had to pay players according to the rules of the agreement they had made before the strike. After 234 days, baseball was finally back.

The season began on April 26. Because it started later than usual, teams played 144 games instead of the usual 162. Right away, it was clear that baseball had a lot of work to do to win back the many fans who were still angry about the strike. Attendance in most ballparks was down. No team had more work to do than the Mariners. They needed a new stadium to replace the Kingdome, but fans in Seattle were tired of watching a losing team year after year.

Most Mariner home games drew crowds of only 12,000 people. The Kingdome could hold more than 50,000. The owners of the team were losing money and the players were told they had to finish first in their division or else the Mariners would move to another city.

"Do you know what kind of pressure that is?" outfielder Jay Buhner told a reporter from *Sports Illustrated*. "Knowing that if you don't win, the team's going to skip town? Man, that's pressure."

A BIG PAIN

Pressure or not, Junior was happy to get back to playing the game he loves. Returning to the field felt sweeter when he and his brother, Craig, played together in an exhibition game during the three–week training period before Opening Day.

During the first three weeks of the season, the Mariners stayed close to first place. Though Junior was batting only .263, he led the team with seven homers. There were signs that he was going to have another monster season. Then Junior broke two bones in his left wrist when he slammed into the centerfield fence after making a spectacular catch in a game against the Orioles on May 26.

Junior's injury was so severe that he needed surgery. Doctors had to use a metal plate and seven screws to hold the broken bones together. Junior was not expected to play again until September.

Without their best player, the Mariners struggled to a 51–49 record by August 15. Their hopes of finishing first in their division were fading when Junior returned to the lineup that day. Junior gave them hope, but the Mariners still lost. Things looked so bleak, the players closed the locker room and held a meeting on August 24, before a game against the Yankees.

That night, the team got fired up. The team was down to its final out in the bottom of the ninth when it rallied for two runs. Junior hit the game–winning home run. After that game, the Mariners were unstoppable.

"That was the one that got us going," manager Lou Piniella told *Sports Illustrated.* "It wasn't just how we did it, but because Junior did it. We had him back."

BACK IN THE GROOVE

The Mariners kept winning and winning and winning. After the final game of the regular season, they were tied with the Angels with a 79–66 record. The two teams met in a one–game playoff in Seattle on October 2. Mariner ace Randy Johnson pitched an overpowering game and Seattle buried the Angels, 9–1. The fans went crazy. The city of Seattle had caught Marinermania.

The Mariners flew to New York the next day to take on the Yankees in the American League Division series. Junior belted a home run in each of the first two games, but the Mariners lost both. The second defeat became a real heartbreaker when Yankee catcher Jim Leyritz hit a game–winning homer in the bottom of the 15th inning.

"Refuse to lose!" signs were hung all over Seattle when the Mariners returned home for the next three games. They were just one defeat away from being eliminated, but they took the slogan to heart. On October 6, Randy Johnson shut down New York, and Junior cracked another homer as the Mariners won, 7–4. The next night, Junior hit another blast as Seattle came back from being down 5–0 to win, 11–8. That set the stage for the incredible fifth and deciding game.

A GAME TO REMEMBER

What a game it was. The Mariners were behind, 4–2, in the eighth inning when Junior set a playoff record by smacking his fifth home run of the series. The shot sparked a rally that let Seattle tie the score. The Yankees scored a run in the top of the 11th, but Seattle simply refused to lose. There were no outs and a runner was on first base in the bottom of the 11th. More than just a game was at stake. The Mariners were chasing a dream.

Junior was the man Mariner fans wanted at bat during that big moment in the 11th inning of the deciding game of the series against New York. He was the best player the team ever had. He had already set an American League playoff record by belting five home runs in the five games (including one earlier in this game) against the Yankees. If he could hit another, the Mariners would be on their way to play the Cleveland Indians in the American League Championship Series.

Junior was ready as Yankee pitcher Jack McDowell wound up and fired. Base hit to centerfield. Runners were now on first and second. Junior had become the potential winning run.

Moments later, Edgar Martinez, the Seattle designated hitter, smacked a hit into leftfield, and Junior took off at top speed. He raced around second and headed for third as the runner ahead of him scored the tying run. Junior kept going. A throw was on its way toward the plate as Junior raced home. The crowd held its breath as Junior slid …

Safe! The Mariners had won, 6–5!

Junior was quickly mobbed by his joyous teammates as the Kingdome exploded with deafening cheers. It was a moment few baseball fans will ever forget.

The Mariners later lost the league championship series to the Indians, but that defeat did not erase the magic of the thrilling game — and series — against the Yankees. The Mariners had become Seattle's heroes at long last. It was only fitting that Junior had been the one who scored the winning run.

THE MAGIC SEASON

Many people feel that game was one of the most exciting ever played. Mariner fans on a flight from

Denver, Colorado, to Seattle that night asked the pilot to keep them informed of the score. When the plane as over the state of Washington, the fans were able to listen to the play–by–play on the headphones because the plane could pick up the radio signal. They could listen in on all the crazy excitement below.

The Kingdome turned into a madhouse after Junior singled and then scored the winning run that night. The fans went crazy and television cameras spotted Junior's smile shining from underneath the pile of happy teammates who buried him at home plate.

"I always wanted to be on the team that is jumping on one another, celebrating," Junior told reporters after the game.

Junior was asked if the victory had been his biggest baseball thrill. "Third biggest," he replied. "Playing in the outfield with my father was first, then playing next to my brother in spring training."

Nine days later, the Cleveland Indians eliminated the Mariners in the league championship series, four games to two. Four days after that, Junior and his wife welcomed a daughter, Taryn, into the family.

The Mariners' magic season was over. Junior would have to wait for his next big league thrill: winning a World Series.

Winning the World Series would mean more to Junior than all the home runs he could ever hit. It would mean that he, too, is a champion.

"If the home runs help us win, fine," Junior told reporters after the big playoff game against the Yankees. "But they don't mean any more than anything else anyone does on our team to help out. Like the homer I hit in the eighth inning, I liked my single in the eleventh more because it was part of the winning rally."

Junior had high hopes that the Mariners would be champions soon.

JUNIOR'S 1995 SEASON

▶ Selected to his sixth straight All-Star starting lineup. He received the second-highest number votes in the American League.

▶ Became the seventh-youngest player to reach 1,000 career hits.

▶ His five home runs in the division series tied Reggie Jackson's major league record for most home runs in a post-season series.

▶ Won his sixth straight Gold Glove award.

CASHING IN

Things were getting a lot better in Seattle. The team and the city had suffered through 18 seasons of failing to finish higher than third place in the American League West division. Finally, in 1995, the Mariners had reached the top. They made it all the way to the American League Championship Series. In 1996, Seattle players and fans had their sights set on one goal: winning the World Series.

Junior had reached a new level in his baseball career. He was continuing to put up impressive numbers, and he was still winning All–Star recognition and Gold Glove awards. But he was also starting to raise the level of play of his teammates. He had changed the Mariners from a losing team into a winning one. And, as any baseball expert will tell you, that is the true mark of a champion.

The Mariners realized how valuable Junior was to their team. They felt he was the best player in baseball.

And Junior was still only 25 years old by the time the 1995 season had ended. He still had many outstanding seasons to come.

The Mariners not only realized how good Junior was, but they also knew that they would need to pay him a lot of money to keep him in Seattle. Money was a problem for the Mariners. The Seattle area has fewer residents than larger cities, like Los Angeles or New York, have. Because fewer people live in the Seattle area, the team doesn't draw as many fans to its games. It also doesn't get as much money from television deals as do teams in bigger cities. Because there are fewer people to watch baseball games in the Seattle area, the television stations can't make as much money from commercials.

AN OFFER HE COULDN'T REFUSE

The Mariners had a big decision to make before the 1996 season. Junior was set to become a free agent at the end of that season. This meant the Mariners had to extend his current contract, or else he would be able to sign with any of the other 27 major league teams.

The Mariners didn't have enough money to pay Junior and still hold on to their other talented players. So they traded first baseman Tino Martinez, third baseman Mike Blowers, and relief pitcher Jeff Nelson to free up some cash. They took that cash and offered it to Junior in a contract extension.

The Mariners weren't sure if Junior would sign the contract extension. After the 1995 season, he had complained about Seattle's cold, damp winters. He was also building a family home on a golf course near Orlando, Florida.

"I like Seattle, the fans and all," Junior said. "But being here in Florida, where we can go outdoors to hang all the time, every day, is great."

The deal the Mariners offered Junior turned out to be too good to pass up. It was a four-year, $34-million extension of his contract. It made Junior the highest-paid player in baseball history at the time. It had an average annual value of $8.5 million. This topped the $7.29 million annual average of the six-year deal Barry Bonds signed with the San Francisco Giants in 1992. The extension started with the 1997 season. That meant Junior was under contract with the Mariners through the 2000 season.

"I cannot tell you how excited the Mariners organization is to have the best player in baseball under contract through the turn of the century," Mariner president Chuck Armstrong said after the signing.

Junior got a signing bonus of $2.5 million. The terms of the contract extension stated that he would be paid $7.25 million in 1997. In 1998, he would get $7.75 million. He would then get $8.25 million in both 1999 and 2000. Junior could also earn bonuses by playing well.

For instance, if he was named Most Valuable Player of the World Series, he would get another $100,000.

Junior was very happy about his new contract. But he was worried about the Mariners. They had traded away some good players. Junior wasn't sure if the 1996 Mariners would be as good as the 1995 team.

"I hated to see us break up a good team and a good bunch of guys," Junior said. "I care a lot about who I play with. It hasn't helped to see Tino, Mike, and Jeff get traded. The guys they're bringing in may be good players, but we just don't know how it will all fit together. It's like we're starting over. The Mariners are always starting over, and that gets old."

AN EARLY-SEASON ROLL

The Mariners may have been starting over, but they started well in 1996. After going 4–4 in their first eight games, the team won eight straight. Their 12–4 record put them back on top in the A.L. West. But that didn't last long.

The Mariners followed their eight-game winning streak with only eight wins in their next 22 games. They found themselves five-and-a-half games behind the Texas Rangers. Junior was hitting home runs, but his batting average was just .241. Some of the fans and local newspapers blamed Junior for the team's struggles. They felt that a player making so much money should be able to lead the team to victory every game.

Junior was not happy about those complaints. "You sign a big contract and if you don't deliver from Day One, they jump all over you," Junior said. "I'm just trying to go up to the plate, swing the bat, and feel comfortable."

The Mariners and their manager, Lou Piniella, didn't panic. The manager blamed Junior's early-season slump on the wrist injury he had suffered in 1995. Mr. Piniella knew it was just a matter of time until Junior would have a hot streak.

"We knew coming out of spring training that it may take a while for Junior's wrist to fully recover," the manager said. "He didn't just break the wrist, he shattered it."

NUMBER 200

Lou Piniella's faith in Junior was rewarded. Junior got at least one hit in seven straight games between May 15 and May 23. In those seven games, he batted .436 with 17 hits in 39 at-bats. The highlight of Junior's seven-game hot streak was a home run he hit off Boston's Vaughn Eshelman on May 21. It was Junior's 11th home run of the season. More important, it was the 200th of his career. Only six players in baseball history had reached 200 career homers at a younger age than Junior. All six of those players are in the Hall of Fame.

"Once Junior got his two-hundreth homer out of the way, he started hitting the ball real well," Lou Piniella said. "That kind of milestone would be on anybody's mind."

How well was Junior swinging the bat? The New York Yankees found out the hard way. On May 24, Junior smacked a two-run homer off Yankee starting pitcher Scott Kamieniecki in the fourth inning. In the sixth inning, Junior drilled a three-run shot off his former teammate, relief pitcher Jeff Nelson. Junior topped off his awesome day with a solo homer off Yankee reliever Steve Howe. For the first time in his pro career, Junior had smacked three home runs in one game!

"That's the first time I've hit three homers in a game since I was in high school," Junior said after the game. "I wasn't even thinking about it."

The Mariners beat the Yankees, 10–4, to move to within two-and-a-half games of the first-place Rangers in the A.L. West. It was the closest the Mariners had been to the Rangers in nearly three weeks. Junior was providing the firepower his team needed. He had raised his batting average to .301 after his four-for-four day against the Yankees. He also set a Mariner team record with five runs scored. He matched a career high with six runs batted in against New York.

"He is special," said Yankee manager Joe Torre. "When he was seventeen or eighteen years old, I heard the rumors about how good he was. All those rumors were true."

Junior was named American League Player of the Week for the seven days from May 20 to May 26. In six games, he batted .462 with five home runs and 14 RBIs. Junior thought his hot hitting was a result of staying more relaxed at the plate.

"I'm not trying to hit the ball seven hundred miles," Junior said. "I'm just going up there to see what's pitched and try to hit it that way and start something."

Junior was so hot that nothing, it seemed, would be able to stop him. But just four weeks later, Junior was stopped.

ON THE DISABLED LIST

The Mariners faced the Toronto Blue Jays for a two-game series in Seattle on July 18 and 19. The Blue Jays were not a very good team, so the Mariners saw it as a chance to make up ground on the first-place Rangers. It turned out to be a disaster.

The Mariners lost both games of the series. They dropped the first game, 11–3, and lost the second game, 9–2. But what was even worse than losing the games was the fact that Seattle lost its best player.

In the third inning of the second game, Junior took a big swing at a pitch from Toronto's Erik Hanson. He fouled the ball back behind the plate. He suddenly dropped his bat and starting walking toward the dugout. Junior was in pain. He was taken to the hospital where X-rays showed that he had fractured the bone where the wrist meets the hand.

"He took an awkward swing," said the Mariner team doctor, Dr. Mitch Storey. Thanks to the force in Junior's swing, the end of the bat handle had snapped off a piece of bone. The bone was at the base of the hand. "He said it just popped," said Dr. Storey.

Junior had surgery the next morning and was placed on the disabled list for the second time in 13 months. Mariner fans feared that Junior might miss as many games as he had when he broke his wrist during the 1995 season. He missed 73 that time. But Mariner doctors assured fans that the injury wasn't nearly as bad.

"It's not a serious injury," said Dr. Storey. "It's relatively common in baseball. His recovery time can be as quick as three weeks. It's nothing like what he went through last year, and he should be back in a short period of time."

Junior wasn't back in time to play in the All-Star Game. He had been elected to his seventh straight All-Star team. He received more than three million votes, which was more than any other major league player. But for the second straight year, Junior missed the game because of an injury.

THE MAN IS BACK

The good news was that Dr. Storey turned out to be right about Junior's injury. It wasn't as serious as the broken wrist in 1995. Junior missed only 20 games this time, and he was back in the Mariner lineup on July 14 for a game against the Angels.

Fans expected Junior to be a little rusty for his first few games back. Boy, were they wrong. Junior smacked a home run and a double in his first game back from the disabled list. He went on to get at least one hit in 13 of

14 games from July 16 to July 30. Junior hit a whopping .386 during those two weeks. Then, on July 31, Junior cracked two home runs in a game against the Milwaukee Brewers. By the time July had ended, Junior had 34 home runs. It was as if he hadn't missed a game all season.

The Mariners continued to play well. Their winning percentage didn't fall below .500 during the entire 1996 season. But the Rangers were playing even better. By September 11, Texas had taken a nine-game lead over Seattle. How could the Mariners make up that much ground? They would have to start winning, and keep winning. And they would have to sweep Texas in an upcoming four-game series.

JUNIOR'S 1996 SEASON

▷ Set Mariner team records with 49 home runs and 140 RBIs.

▷ Led the majors in All-Star votes (3,064,814) while being elected to his seventh straight All-Star team.

▷ Became seventh-youngest player to reach 200 career home runs.

▷ Won his seventh straight Gold Glove award.

Junior and the Mariners rose to the challenge. First, they won four games against other teams. Then, they defeated the Rangers in four straight games in Seattle. The scores were 6–0, 5–2, 5–2, and 7–6.

The Oakland A's came to town the night after the Rangers series. Seattle continued its winning ways. Junior broke his own team record for most home runs in one season by hitting his 46th homer of the season in a 12–2 win over Oakland. After that game, the Mariners were within one game of the first–place Rangers. It was Seattle's ninth win in a row. In just nine days, the Mariners had made up eight games on Texas in the standings.

But 1996 would not turn out to be the Mariners' year. After winning two games against Oakland, they lost three games in a row. They won again, only to lose two more. They had run out of gas in the end. They fell short in their bid for the American League West crown. The team and its fans were disappointed, but at the same time they were encouraged by the great comeback that had fallen short.

HUGE NUMBERS

Junior had enjoyed his best season yet. His .303 batting average marked the sixth time in seven seasons that he had hit at least .300. His 49 home runs had him in third place in the American League. It also set a Mariner team record. Junior's 140 RBIs, 125 runs scored, and .628 slugging percentage all ranked fifth among A.L. players. Junior won his seventh Gold Glove and finished fourth in the voting for A.L. Most Valuable Player. And he did it all despite missing 20 games due to his injury.

The Mariners and their fans were very pleased with Junior's 1996 season. Even though he had signed his big contract extension before the season, he had continued to work hard to improve his game. The Mariners still thought that Junior was the best player in baseball. He would use the 1997 season to prove them right.

MVP

The 1997 season started with a bang for Junior and the Mariners. The defending world champion New York Yankees visited Seattle for Opening Night. A sellout crowd of 57,586 screaming fans filled the Kingdome to see their Mariners battle Yankee ace pitcher David Cone. Junior and his teammates wanted to make sure the fans went home happy.

The Yankees jumped out to a 1–0 lead with a run in the top of the first inning. But that lead did not last long. With two outs in the bottom of the first, Junior crushed a pitch 421 feet into the right–centerfield seats to tie the game. The crowd went wild.

"Some games you get up for, and some you don't," Junior said. "With them winning the World Series and it being Opening Day, if you can't get up for this one, you can't get up at all."

The Yankees took a 2–1 lead with a run in the top of the second inning. But the Mariners battled back.

Mariner third baseman Russ Davis tied the score with a solo homer to lead off the bottom of the third inning. Then, with shortstop Alex Rodriguez on first base, Junior came to bat. He went to a full count of three balls and two strikes against David Cone. David threw Junior a pitch down around his knees. Junior lifted the ball high into the air down the rightfield line. Yankee rightfielder Paul O'Neill drifted back to the warning track. He went all the way back to the wall and looked up . . . it was a home run.

"Right off the bat, I thought I had it," Paul said. "Up to the last second I thought I had it. But it doesn't matter how far it gets out. When it's out, it's a couple of runs." Junior's 327–foot home run had given the Mariners a 4–2 lead.

"I was just trying to see who caught it, Paul O'Neill, the wall, or a fan," Junior said. "I was glad it was the fan."

Neither team scored any more runs the rest of the night. The Mariners had beaten the defending world champions. It was the perfect way to start a new season. And it was Junior who had led the team to victory.

"Junior is amazing. He rises to an occasion as well as anybody I've ever seen," said Mariner manager Lou Piniella. "He's got tremendous skills. When he swings at strikes, he can do anything with the bat. He did it tonight against an excellent pitcher in David Cone. To hit two balls out of the park against him is saying something.

"I know people come to our stadium and expect heroics like this from Junior every night. They know he's still young and might do even more. But to me, Junior is at a point of his career that all he has to do is maintain. He doesn't have to make it better. He's good enough," Lou said.

Yankee manager Joe Torre agreed.

"You pay your money to watch him," Joe said. "You love to watch him play. If I wasn't wearing this [Yankee] uniform, I would have enjoyed it more."

Although it was only the first game of the season, fans and the media wanted to start talking about baseball's home-run record. No one had come close to hitting 61 home runs since Yankee slugger Roger Maris set the record back in 1961. People had started to talk about it in the strike-shortened 1994 season. Now, in 1997, Junior had as good a shot as anybody to break the record, but he just wanted to stay focused on winning games. "I don't even worry about it," Junior said about the record. "I go up there day by day and see what happens. I want to do what the Yankees did last year: win a World Series."

TAKING THE ROCKET DEEP

The Mariners went 13–8 in their first 21 games to take hold of first place in the A.L. West. On April 25, they traveled to Toronto for a three-game series against the

Blue Jays. The Blue Jays had signed star pitcher Roger Clemens before the 1997 season. Roger was scheduled to pitch the first game of the series.

Junior was swinging a hot bat when the Mariners arrived in Toronto. He had 10 home runs in the team's first 21 games. He needed just one more to tie the major league record for most home runs in the month of April. But Junior would have his work cut out for him against a tough pitcher like Roger.

"Roger challenges you, every at-bat," Junior said. "I don't like to leave anything on the field, he doesn't like to leave anything on the mound."

In the third inning, Junior didn't leave anything in the park. He blasted one of Roger's pitches 449 feet into the fourth deck of the Toronto SkyDome. It was Junior's 11th home run of the season. That tied the record for most homers in the month of April.

Three innings later, Junior faced Roger again. This time, he hit a home run to left centerfield. Junior had set a record for homers in April. But the Mariners still trailed in the game, 7–6.

Russ Davis came off the bench to pinch-hit in the eighth inning. With one runner on base, Russ hit a home run to put the Mariners ahead, 8–7. Later in the inning, Junior smacked a home run off Blue Jay relief pitcher Mike Timlin. It was Junior's third home run of the game. The Mariners went on to win, 13–8.

NUMBER 250

"Thirteen home runs in a month? That's more than I ever hit in a year!" said Lou Piniella. (He played in the majors for more than 17 years for four different teams.)

Russ added, "Junior is some kind of special hitter. I've never seen anyone like him."

Junior was happy with his performance. But he was quick to give his teammates some credit for the win.

"Hitting three home runs in a game is special," Junior said. "The record [for most homers in April] is nice, too. But Russ's home run was the biggest. If I hit three and we lose, it spoils it."

Not only did Junior's second home run of the game break the major league record for April homers, but it was the 250th home run of his career. It made Junior the fourth-youngest player in history to reach 250 home runs. Even more amazing: He did it despite missing more than 200 games because of injuries and the 1994 baseball strike.

"I ran out of adjectives for Junior long ago," his manager said.

POWERING THE MARINERS

As Junior continued to slug home runs, pressure continued to build. It seemed as if the only thing the media wanted to discuss was whether Junior would be able to break Roger Maris's home-run record. Junior finished May with 24 home runs, breaking his own record for most homers through May.

Junior hit his 25th homer on June 2 against the Blue Jays. That matched Hall of Famer Jimmie Foxx's mark for second-quickest 25 home runs in a season. Only Babe Ruth hit 25 home runs in fewer games. He did it on June 17, 1928.

On July 5, Junior smacked his 30th home run to become only the third player to have two seasons with at least 30 homers before the All-Star break. (Retired sluggers Mark McGwire and Hall of Famer Willie Stargell are the others.) Fans continued to cheer for Junior, and they elected him to his eighth All-Star team. He led the majors in voting for the third time.

By the end of August, Junior appeared to have fallen off the pace to break the home-run record. He had 43 home runs entering the Mariners' August 31 game at Los Angeles. That meant Junior needed 18 homers in his last 25 games just to tie Roger Maris. In the meantime, the Mariners were in a tight race in the A.L. West. They held a slim one-game lead over the Anaheim Angels.

Junior realized how important the remaining games were for the Mariners. He also knew that, as the star of the team, it was up to him to provide the power. Junior came through. On August 31, he hit a key homer, his

44th of the year. It was in the Mariners' 3–1 extra–inning win over the Los Angeles Dodgers. The win snapped the team's four–game losing streak. It kept the Mariners one game ahead of the Angels in the A.L. West.

NUMBER 50

Junior's homer against the Dodgers started one of the hottest streaks of his career. He homered twice the next night in a 9–6 win over the Padres. He had another two–homer game on September 4, when Seattle beat the Minnesota Twins, 9–6. The hot streak continued with a home run against the Twins on September 7. It was the seventh home run Junior had hit in seven days. The home run was Junior's 50th of the season. Only 17 players had hit 50 homers in one season. But he didn't feel much like celebrating. This time, the Mariners *lost* the game, 9–6.

"I'd rather have the win," Junior said. "This is not about personal bests. I want to win the World Series. Whatever it takes to get that, I'll try to do."

Lou Piniella was not happy about losing the game, but he also realized the importance of hitting 50 home runs in a season.

"Fifty is a lot of home runs," the manager said. "Only a few players have ever hit that many. It's quite a feat. He's quite a player."

Junior's awesome home-run streak proved to be a big help for the Mariner playoff hopes. During his seven-day streak, Seattle gained three games on Anaheim in the standings. The Mariners led the Angels by four games and had only 19 games remaining in the season. But Junior knew that there was still plenty of work to be done.

"The season is not over yet," he said. "We have to win more games. I just want to help win games."

Winning games is exactly what the Mariners did. After a loss to the Kansas City Royals on September 8, Seattle won 10 of its next 14 games to clinch the A.L. West title.

PLAYOFFS BOUND

By the time the 1997 season ended, the Mariners had won 90 games to set a franchise record. Junior led the American League with 56 home runs and 147 runs batted in. His 56 homers were the seventh-most in major league history.

But Junior and the Mariners had no time to celebrate. They faced a difficult challenge in the playoffs. They were matched up with the Baltimore Orioles in a best-of-five playoff series. The Orioles had won 98 games in 1997 and had the best record in the American League.

The Mariners sent their ace pitcher, Randy Johnson, to the mound for the first game of the series against the Orioles. The Orioles countered with an ace pitcher of their own, Mike Mussina. Baltimore had Randy's number that day, and came away with a 9–3 win. The next night was like an instant replay. The Orioles won again by a score of 9–3.

The Mariners came back to win the third game of the series, 4–2. Randy Johnson was back on the mound for Game 4, but Mike Mussina turned out to be too much for the Mariner batters. The O's won, 3–1. They had ended the Mariners' season by defeating Seattle, three games to one. Junior had only two hits and no homers in 15 at-bats during the series.

JUNIOR'S 1997 SEASON

▷ Became the first Mariner player ever to be named American League MVP.

▷ Led the A.L. with 56 home runs and 147 RBIs (both Mariner records).

▷ Broke his own major league record for most home runs through the end of May (24).

▷ Elected to his eighth All-Star Game and led the majors in voting for the third time.

Mariner players and fans were disappointed in the team's loss. They had thought that this might be the year the Mariners went all the way to the World Series. Instead, they were forced to wait another year.

MR. MVP

The heartbreaking loss to the Orioles could not take away from Junior's awesome season. In November, he was named the American League's Most Valuable Player. The vote was unanimous: Every sportswriter who got to vote picked Junior for MVP.

"It means a lot to me," Junior said. "It's a great award, and I don't know what to say or how to say it. I've never been in this situation."

Ken, Sr. never won an MVP award during his baseball career. He knew how hard it was to win. And he was very proud of Junior for being named MVP.

"I am, without a doubt, the happiest man in the world," Ken, Sr. said. "Winning the MVP is a special thing. I know how special, because I tried with all my might and ability to be worthy of one myself."

He may not have ever won an MVP, but Ken, Sr. had won something more important: a World Series.

"Dad has those three World Series rings over me," Junior said. "Hopefully, I'll get one next year. The MVP doesn't give me any bragging rights over him. He still has the Series trophies."

Junior was then asked if winning the MVP award took at least some of the sting out of losing to the Orioles in the playoffs.

"No. I've always said that I want to be a part of a winning tradition, and we're headed in the right direction," Junior said. "We just fell short this year. Hopefully, we'll be back next year."

A 50/50 CHANCE

When the 1998 season began, the Mariners had high hopes. They were the defending American League West champions. Junior was coming off the best season of his career.

But the Mariners struggled to get on track. Their pitchers performed so poorly over the first two weeks that the team fired its pitching coach just 11 games into the season. The day after the coach was fired, the Mariner bullpen blew a game against the Indians. Cleveland rallied for six runs in the sixth inning for a 6–5 victory. The loss was Seattle's sixth in a row, and it dropped the team's record to 3–9. That matched the worst start in club history.

The loss to the Indians also ruined a great game for Junior. He smacked two home runs, including the 300th of his career. Junior became the second-youngest player ever to hit 300 career home runs. He was 28 years, five months old. Jimmie Foxx was about six months younger than that when he hit his 300th career homer in 1935.

JUNIOR'S 1998 SEASON

- Became the first major league player to hit 350 home runs before turning 29.
- Joined Babe Ruth and Mark McGwire as the only three players to hit 50 or more home runs in two straight seasons.
- Won the All-Star Home Run Derby by smacking 19 in the three-round competition.
- Joined Willie Mays and Brady Anderson as the only three players to hit 50 or more homers and steal 20 or more bases in the same season.

GOODBYE, KINGDOME

Things were looking up for the Mariners in 1999. Safeco Field, their brand–new home, was being built next to the Kingdome. Safeco was an outdoor stadium with real grass, unlike the Mariners' old home.

The Mariners were scheduled to begin the 1999 season in the Kingdome, before moving to Safeco Field in July. Few people were upset with the move. For 23 years, the Kingdome had been one of the worst stadiums in the majors. "Ugly" and "depressing" were two of the nicer words people used to describe it! It had no charm like Boston's Fenway Park or Chicago's Wrigley Field. Nor did it have a great history like New York's Yankee Stadium.

On April 29, Junior blasted the 11th grand slam of his career as Seattle whipped the Tigers, 22–6, at the Kingdome. It was the most runs the Mariners had ever scored in a game. Junior had six RBIs to tie his career high. The next night, he hit another grand slam to help Seattle beat Toronto, 11–9. Hitting grand slams in two consecutive games was something only 27 other players in major league history had ever accomplished. Junior finished the month of April with nine home runs, 24 RBIs, and a .301 batting average.

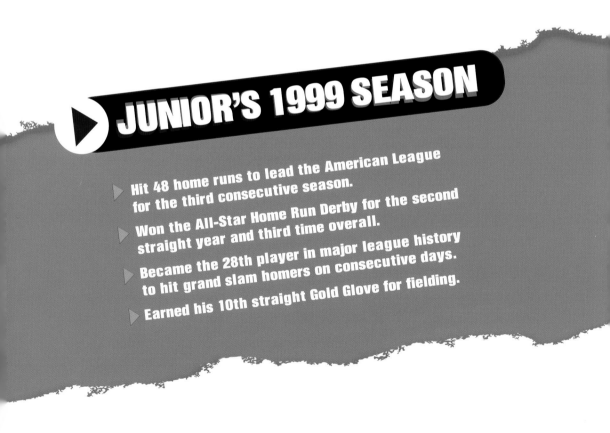

JUNIOR'S 1999 SEASON

- Hit 48 home runs to lead the American League for the third consecutive season.
- Won the All-Star Home Run Derby for the second straight year and third time overall.
- Became the 28th player in major league history to hit grand slam homers on consecutive days.
- Earned his 10th straight Gold Glove for fielding.

May was even better. Junior reeled off a 16-game hitting streak from May 10 to 28. It was the longest streak of his career, but still far short of the major league record. Joe DiMaggio of the New York Yankees had at least one hit in 56 consecutive games during the 1941 season. It's a record that will probably never be broken. Nonetheless, Junior's streak was impressive. He had 27 hits in 63 at-bats (a .429 batting average) during those 16 games, with eight homers and 21 RBIs.

Seattle played its last game at the Kingdome on June 27, against Texas. Junior said good-bye to the big concrete dome by smacking a homer off Aaron Sele. It was the last homer hit in the Kingdome. It was fitting that it came off the bat of the greatest player in Mariner history. Junior later robbed Ranger slugger Juan Gonzalez of a homer by making a leaping catch in center field. The Mariners won, 5–2.

THE BIG FADE

Junior and the Mariners played their first game at Safeco Field on July 15 against the San Diego Padres. Fans loved Safeco, and so did the pitchers. Balls didn't carry as far outdoors as they did indoors. But it took some adjustment for the hitters. Junior struggled and his frustration grew. He hit just .255 after the All-Star break, with 19 homers and 53 RBIs. The Mariners faded down the stretch and finished 16 games behind first-place Texas in the American League West.

It was disappointing, but Junior still had a terrific year. He hit 48 home runs to lead the American League. He finished third with 134 RBIs. He also stole a career-high 24 bases and won his 10th Gold Glove Award.

But Junior knew that he no longer wanted to play in Seattle. He needed a change. The Mariners weren't winning, and he didn't like Safeco Field. He had only one more season left on his contract. Though the Mariners offered him a lot of money to sign a new one, Junior said no. Instead, he asked to be traded. He wanted to play in a city that is closer to Orlando, Florida, where he and his family lived during the winter. Or better yet, he wanted to be traded to his old hometown of Cincinnati, Ohio, where his dad was a coach.

CINCINNATI BOUND

When the word got out that Junior wanted a trade, it didn't take long for teams to start calling the Mariners. The Braves called. So did the Yankees. The Mets even worked out a trade with Seattle, but according to major league rules, Junior had the right to veto any deal. Players with 10 years of major league experience, and five with the same team, have that right. Junior didn't want to play in New York. The deal was off.

Junior then told the Mariners he would only accept a trade to Cincinnati. The Reds were a good team. They had won 96 games in 1999, just missing the playoffs.

Junior said that if the Mariners didn't send him to Cincinnati, he'd return to Seattle, play out the final season of his contract, and leave as a free agent after the 2000 season. The Mariners were stuck. They had to work out a deal with the Reds or lose their best player and get nothing in return.

A deal was hammered out and the trade was completed on February 10. Junior was sent to the Reds for outfielder Mike Cameron, infielder Antonio Perez, and pitchers Brett Tomko and Jake Meyer. Junior was going home and would be with his dad again.

>> LIFE IN CINCINNATI

From the moment Junior signed with the Reds on February 10, 2000, everyone knew he would be front-page news. When Junior showed up at the Reds' spring training camp in Sarasota, Florida later in February, dozens of reporters were there to cover his arrival.

Junior quietly reported to camp, but he was followed everywhere he went. About 100 reporters and photographers were present. "I just figured I'd sneak into the locker room without being noticed and go onto the field and that's it. I didn't have any idea there would be this many people and cameras here," he said.

So much attention made the quiet superstar uncomfortable. "Nervous? Not at all. My legs aren't shaking," Junior joked during a press conference, as he pointed to his jumping right heel.

A couple of days later, fans got a chance to see Junior in his first full-squad workout with the Reds. About 2,000 people — more than twice the crowd at

the last workout before Junior arrived — pressed against the fences to see him take his cuts in the batting cage. People started lining up to get a glimpse of Junior two-and-a-half hours before the gates opened. "It's a little tough," Junior said of the pre-season attention. "I hope things will become normal, to a certain extent. I don't want to disrupt the club at all."

UPS AND DOWNS

Junior's first season in Cincinnati had its shares of highs and lows. Throughout the season, he was bothered by knee and hamstring injuries. Although Junior was voted to the All-Star Game lineup for the 11th straight season, he didn't play in the game. Junior had hurt his right knee against the Arizona Diamondbacks and had to sit out the All-Star Game to rest up. Ken wore a protective knee brace to help the healing process.

On September 11, Junior tore up his left hamstring when he crashed into Chicago Cubs' catcher Joe Girardi while trying to score. Junior had to be helped from the field. At first, it was thought that Junior would be out of action for only a few days. Unfortunately, the injury was more serious than doctors thought. Junior did not start another game for the rest of the season. After the injury, Junior made only three pinch-hitting appearances, hitting his 40th home run in one of them.

Despite the injury, Junior lit up the 2000 season with plenty of fireworks. In the 145 games he played, Junior led the Reds in homers (40), RBIs (118), runs scored (100), total bases (289), and walks (94). He knocked in 100 RBIs for the fifth straight season, and eighth time in his career.

After a slow start, Junior had begun to hit for a big average. In his first 96 games, Junior batted only .235. But in his last 49 games he batted .337, including .327 in August and .385 in September. Junior also put together two 11–game hitting streaks, batting .357 in his first streak in June, and .333 in a late–July to early–August streak.

JUNIOR'S 2000 SEASON

▷ Led the Reds in homers, RBIs, runs scored, total bases, and walks.

▷ Elected to his 11th All-Star Game.

▷ Had his fifth straight 100 RBI season.

▷ Became only the fourth player in history to hit 40 homers in five straight seasons.

▷ Became only the fourth player in history to hit 40 homers in both leagues.

INSTANT DIVIDENDS

Junior's home runs paid off handsomely for the Reds. The team had a record of 24–11 when he homered and 18 of his 40 dingers tied games or put the Reds ahead. However, the Reds dropped to an 85–77 record, winning 11 fewer games than they did in 1999. They finished second in the National League Central Division.

Junior's first year with Cincinnati had been one to remember. But little did Junior know that disappointment was on its way in 2001.

A PAINFUL START

The 2001 season spelled T–R–O–U–B–L–E for Junior and the Reds right from the beginning. In a spring training game against the Kansas City Royals, Junior strained his left hamstring while rounding third base as he was heading home. Junior pulled up sharply, fell on his back, and grabbed his leg in pain. The same bad hamstring that knocked him out of action the previous September was injured once again.

It was decided that Junior would sit out the remaining spring training games. Junior and Reds' manager Bob Boone were hopeful that the centerfielder would be ready for Opening Day against the Atlanta Braves the next week. But it wasn't to be. Boone had to drop Junior's name from the Opening Day lineup in order to give his star time to heal.

"If it's [the injury] going to mean me missing a couple of games, I'd rather do it now than have it like last year. I'd rather take care of the problem now," Junior said.

MR. PINCH HITTER

The team decided to keep Junior out of the starting lineup indefinitely, rather than place him on the disabled list. Junior doesn't like missing games and believed he could still contribute to the team even with his painful hamstring injury. He was given pinch–hitting chores early in 2001.

In late April, Junior aggravated his hamstring in a pinch–hitting appearance against the Colorado Rockies while running out of the batter's box. That was it for Junior. On April 29, he was placed on the disabled list for the first time since 1995. "Why take a chance at this point? We tried something [using Junior as a pinch hitter], it didn't work," said team medical director Dr. Timothy Kremchek. Junior's stats up to that time read 0–for–12 with three walks as a pinch hitter.

Junior sat out the next six weeks, giving the injury time to heal while exercising to strengthen the hamstring. Junior remained optimistic and knew that he'd be ready for full–time action when he could run without a problem.

TEAM WOES

Junior's injury wasn't the only headache bothering the Reds: The team was losing ballgames at an alarming pace. After posting a respectable 14–10 record in April, the Reds went 6–22 in May. The 22 losses were a franchise record for the month of May and were the most team losses in any month since July 1952. In addition to Junior's bad hamstring, injuries to shortstop Barry Larkin, third baseman Aaron Boone (manager Bob Boone's son), and pitchers Scott Williamson and Pete Harnisch, hurt the team badly. By the time Junior returned to the lineup, the Reds were a very poor 25–40.

But Junior finally *did* get back on the field on June 16, going 1–for–3 with a single against the Rockies. Bob Boone knew it was going to take Junior some time to feel totally comfortable once again. "It's spring training time for him . . . When he realizes that he can run and the leg won't fall off, he'll be more natural and just play," Bob said.

Junior cracked his first home run of the 2001 season on June 19 against the Milwaukee Brewers in a losing effort. (Junior's last home run had been on September 19, 2000!) In his first five games back, Junior was 7–for–18, with one homer and five RBIs. But the Reds continued to stumble in June and July and the frustration of his injury and the team's poor performance began to show on Junior.

THE NEED TO WIN

In late July, Junior was quoted as saying, "This year has been messed up for me since Day One." After that, Junior suggested to a reporter from the *Cincinnati Enquirer* that he was considering retirement. When the story came out, Junior said his comments were misinterpreted or made in jest. But Junior cleared the air about retiring — and it was all related to his nagging injury. "I'm not going to be sitting around for six or seven years with a hamstring injury to collect a check. That's not what I'm about," he said.

However, there was no denying that Junior was disappointed that the Reds had traded three veteran players to save money and get younger prospects. "I want to win and I don't want to see a bunch of good players on this team go somewhere else and win . . . When you get over thirty [years old], you never know how long your career

JUNIOR'S 2001 SEASON

▶ Led Reds with 22 homers.
▶ Hit his third career inside-the-park home run.
▶ Had his fewest plate appearances since 1995.

is going to be . . . If they [the Reds] start rebuilding, that means I'm probably going to be one of the guys to go," Junior said.

Junior found his groove in August when he put everyone on notice that the Master Blaster was back. Against the San Francisco Giants on August 9, Junior became the youngest player to reach 450 career home runs when he crushed a Russ Ortiz pitch over the right field wall in Cincinnati. Junior was 31 years 261 days old when he hit the historic blast — 15 days younger than Jimmie Foxx. Junior was unstoppable in August, pounding 11 homers with 29 RBIs.

Junior managed to put up very respectable numbers despite his injuries. In only 111 games, he led the Reds with 22 homers. His .286 batting average was his personal best since 1997. However, the Reds sank to a 66–96 record while Junior's former team, the Mariners, were on their way to setting the American League record for most wins in a season (116).

CLOSER TO THE RECORD

Junior was only 32 years old when the 2002 season began. If he remains healthy, there's no telling how many major league records he will own by the time his career is over. He has already accomplished more than most players do during their entire careers. With every home run Junior hits, he comes closer and closer to the greatest record in all of sports: Hank Aaron's 755 career home runs.

If Junior can average 45 home runs a season for the rest of his career, he'll break Hammerin' Hank's record during the 2008 season. He will be 39 years old. But Junior isn't thinking about breaking Hank Aaron's or anybody else's record. To him, winning a World Series would mean more than all the home runs he could ever hit. It would mean that Junior, like his dad, is a champion.

No matter what happens, Junior knows what he wants in the end. "When I'm done playing," he says, "I want people to say about me, 'He could flat-out play. He had fun while he played, and I enjoyed watching him play.' That's all. I don't think about being the next Willie Mays. I just want to be the best player that I can be as Ken Griffey, Junior."

NEWSFLASH!

On April 7, 2002, Ken injured his right knee in a rundown play between third base and home plate. The injury, coming in only the Red's sixth game of the season, was serious. Ken was forced to go on the disabled list. At press time, it was not known when he would return to the lineup.

CAREER STATS

Year	Team	Games	AB	R	H	2B	3B	HR	RBI	AVG
1989	Seattle	127	455	61	120	23	0	16	61	.264
1990	Seattle	155	597	91	179	28	7	22	80	.300
1991	Seattle	154	548	76	179	42	1	22	100	.327
1992	Seattle	142	565	83	174	39	4	27	103	.308
1993	Seattle	156	582	113	180	38	3	45	109	.309
1994	Seattle	111	433	94	140	24	4	40	90	.323
1995	Seattle	72	260	52	67	7	0	17	42	.258
1996	Seattle	140	545	125	165	26	2	49	140	.303
1997	Seattle	157	608	125	185	34	3	56	147	.304
1998	Seattle	161	633	120	180	33	3	56	146	.284
1999	Seattle	160	606	123	173	26	3	48	134	.285
2000	Cincinnati	145	520	100	141	22	3	40	118	.271
2001	Cincinnati	111	364	57	104	20	2	22	65	.286
CAREER TOTALS		1,791	6,716	1,220	1,987	362	35	460	1,335	.296

GLOSSARY

dingers home runs

frustration feelings of discouragement

glimpse a brief look at something

hamstring one of the two large tendons at the back of a person's knee

momentum the force or speed of motion

recognition attention or favorable notice

RESOURCES

Books

Gutman, Bill. *Ken Griffey, Jr.: Baseball's Best.* Brookfield, CT: Millbrook Press, 1998.

Staff of Sports Publishing, Inc. *101 Little Known Facts About Ken Griffey, Jr.* Champaign, IL: Sagamore Publishing, 1997.

Magazine

SPORTS ILLUSTRATED FOR KIDS
135 W. 50th Street
New York, NY 10020
(800) 992–0196
http://www.sikids.com

Web Sites

The Official Site of Major League Baseball
http://www.mlb.com
Learn about your favorite teams and players. This site has all of the up–to–date standings, scores, and statistics. You will also find video highlights, feature articles, links to all major league team pages, and player biographies.

RESOURCES

SPORTS ILLUSTRATED FOR KIDS
http://www.sikids.com
Check out the latest sports news, cool games, and much more.

Organization
National Baseball Hall of Fame and Museum
25 Main Street
P.O. Box 590
Cooperstown, NY 13326
Phone: (888) 425–5633
Fax: (607) 547–2044
http://www.baseballhalloffame.org

INDEX